Contents

Contents

ONE

Taking the Mystery Out of Our Emotions

SOMETIMES LIFE CAN seem like a carnival—exciting but also a bit frightening. The newness, noise, and endless variety of impressions all demand our attention at once. Our senses are bombarded by sideshow barkers and game attendants; the lights, colors, and smells all cry out, "Come to me-me." Our lives are barraged by a seemingly endless variety of ideas, directions, and advice. To whom do we listen? To the voice that shouts the loudest or to the one that speaks the truth? And what is the truth? What is the voice of God?

In the midst of this confusion, many of us resort to patching together odds and ends of advice from women's magazines, helpful hints from newspaper columnists, and insights from scripture. This patched-together approach to life is a hazardous and fragile way to seek guidance. Have you noticed that the advice given one week on a television talk show is only contradicted by next week's women's magazine?

At some point we must decide who we *are* going to listen to. Straddling the fence, leaning first one way then another, brings little emotional or spiritual peace. Once we decide to listen to God's voice, let's stick to that decision long enough to see what kind of fruit it will bear, remembering that "every sound tree bears good fruit, but the bad tree bears evil fruit. . . . Thus will you know them by their fruit" (Mt 7:17, 20).

If we base our lives on the Lord and his word to us in

scripture, we will experience a harmony and a stability that won't give way beneath us. Instead, it will provide a secure springboard for further growth. Unlike many modern prescriptions for health and well-being, the Lord's wisdom does not change from month to month. We need to follow his way, discarding advice and approaches that contradict or undermine his word to us. Our emotions are no different than any other area of our lives. The Lord is the Lord; he can be trusted with every facet of our lives, including our emotions.

This book is based on the assumption that Christian women are willing and eager to listen to the voice of the Lord as they seek to strengthen their emotional lives and to overcome some specific emotional difficulties. Before this can happen each woman must decide to embrace scripture and the wisdom of Christian tradition as truth for her life today. The wisdom that God gives is not dated. It provides strength for living in the twentieth century just as it did for living in the first century or the fifteenth. The Lord's way is the best and surest way for anyone to travel. He is a Father who loves and cares for his daughters, who wants to provide the fullness of life for them.

Tools for Good

Our emotions are meant to be tools to aid us in our Christian lives. God has given us his word in scripture to help us evaluate how well those tools are working. And he has provided other helps for us as well. The wonderful gift of repentance and forgiveness, the strength that comes from inner healing and deliverance from evil spirits, the power of the Holy Spirit, the freedom of self-discipline, and the love of other Christians are just some of the tools that God has put at our disposal to help us live that whole and holy life to which he calls us.

How are these tools to operate in our lives as women? It is essential to consider how we experience our emotions as women. After all, women are different from men, aren't they? I've been frustrated more than once by advice given by well-meaning Christian authors or teachers. Certainly they have much to offer us, but their advice often lacks an essential feminine perspective, one that draws from the experience of women themselves.

What does scripture say about our emotions? What part does tradition, handed down by the Christian churches, play in our lives today? More specifically, how does a *Christian woman* experience and handle her emotions? After teaching and counselling women for the past twelve years, I'm convinced that the feminine difference *can* be verbalized. Let's leave the carnival, and all the voices clamoring for our attention, to spend some time understanding ourselves as Christian women.

The Emotional Chain Reaction

A unique, but often overlooked, facet of a woman's emotional life is what I call the emotional chain reaction. Women often experience their emotions not just one at a time but in a series or all at once. Often, one emotion gives birth to another and then another, with each succeeding emotion generating yet new emotions. This stockpile effect is more common among women than men, though men may experience this to some extent. Some women may have recognized this chain reaction in their lives, but many others haven't the slightest idea that their emotions operate this way. Recognizing this chain reaction can help us understand why we feel and behave the way we do.

For instance, suppose one day that you wake up a bit late. Rushing to get ready for work, you find that the sink is plugged. After fooling with it for fifteen minutes, you succeed in unplugging it. Finally you are able to wash up. Your irritation and frustration mount as you slam the door, racing to get to the office on time.

A co-worker had promised to have some information ready that you needed. But when you arrive, you find an apologetic note from her, saying that she wasn't able to get the information you wanted. Angry now, you think some very harsh thoughts about her abilities and stamp into her office demanding a full explanation. Later that afternoon, feelings of regret and condemnation surge in you as your anger recedes. Guilt and self-condemnation torment you for the remainder of the day. That evening you feel depressed and angry for the very unchristian way you handled the situation. When you try to pray, the Lord seems far away.

Let's take a look at what happened. First, irritability made way for anger, which then gave way to guilt and condemnation. Later, depression and self-anger became two more links of the chain. Unless you understand that your emotions can become linked, you will deal with the symptoms as though they are the disease. Difficulty with self-anger and depression are not the problem—they're just a clue. If you take a few moments to "play detective" in order to track down the original source of these emotions, you will be able to deal more effectively with them.

Four Equals One?

All too often we try to dissect our emotions, to examine them under a magnifying glass in order to find out how we are *really* doing. My experience with women, particularly, is that we operate as an integrated whole, not as a collection of specialized units, independent of one another. It is impossible to have an accurate picture of a woman unless we view her as a person who has a body, mind, self-image, relationship with the Lord, and emotions. We get a lopsided picture when we relate to only one aspect of ourselves or other women.

If we are to stand strong and secure in the Lord, we will need to have four foundation stones in place. First of all, Jesus Christ is the cornerstone for our emotional health and stability. He is the only one who can save us—from ourselves and our sin. It is impossible to present a Christian approach to the emotions without recognizing that Jesus is the cornerstone.

In addition to the cornerstone, our building will need three other foundation stones. One of these is our mind, the gateway to our emotions. Another is our self-image. How we feel about ourselves and how we think others see us is crucial. The third and last foundation stone concerns our knowledge of our physical nature—our bodily makeup—and its effect on our emotions, our relationship with the Lord, and the way we think about ourselves.

So, realizing that Jesus is the cornerstone and that our mind, our self-image, and our physical self are the foundation stones for emotional stability, we can begin to attain the maturity we all desire. If these four aspects are working right, we are stronger for it. If one of them is malfunctioning, our growth toward holiness is inhibited. Once we have laid the foundation, we can deal effectively with specific areas of our emotions that may be giving us trouble.

The first half of this book, then, will lay these foundation stones. The second half will focus on developing the proper perspective on such emotions as depression, anger, guilt, fear, and anxiety. Our goal is not to ignore or repress our emotions, but to make them work for us towards righteous living. The fact that we are Christians fuels our desire for a stable emotional life. We know that our lives will be more peaceful as a result. And the more our emotional lives are in order, the freer we will be to love and serve God and his people.

God has given us our emotions to help us, not to tear us down. They are to be a strength for our lives. Let's take the mystery out of them so they can operate in a way that gives peace to our lives.

Lord, I want my emotions to support my life with you. Show me your plan for my feelings and give me the vision and help I need to put them under your Lordship.

TWO

Jesus Is the Cornerstone

A NY STRUCTURE EXPECTED to stand and endure must be built solidly. A high-rise apartment building should be able to survive rain, high winds, blizzards, and other possible hazards. Without a good foundation, even the strongest and best-constructed upper floors will not be able to withstand the constant buffeting that comes from the elements and from normal daily use.

If we are to have a stable emotional life, one that will endure the wear and tear of daily life, our foundation can only be Jesus Christ. No one can take the place of Jesus as the cornerstone of our lives. "Every one then who hears these words of mine and does them will be like a wise man who built his house upon the rock; and the rain fell, and the floods came, and the winds blew and beat upon that house, but it did not fall, because it had been founded on the rock" (Mt 7:24-25). "For no other foundation can any one lay than that which is laid, which is Jesus Christ" (1 Cor 3:11).

It is well worth the time and energy we invest in nurturing our relationship with God through his Son Jesus Christ. Nothing can be more important in our lives than knowing God and yielding completely to his love. Let us quiet the clamor of our concerns—of money, children, jobs, and the future—to make space in our minds and hearts to understand God more fully, to know the place that he should occupy in our lives. And let us consider what are the ingredients of a committed Christian life.

A Real Relationship

"In this is love, not that we loved God but that he loved us and sent his Son to be the expiation for our sins" (1 Jn 4:10). The key to our relationship with God is that it is primarily a *relationship*. He first loved us and gave us his Son on the cross while we were yet sinners and unworthy of that relationship (Rom 5:8). Jesus' death and resurrection form the basis of our faith as Christians. He alone bridged the gap between God and man so that the family bonds between God and his people could be restored. Through Jesus, we have become daughters of God. We are not slaves or strangers, but daughters. Hallelujah! It's important to remember this, to take it in. Try saying, "God *my* Father, sent his only son Jesus to die for *me* because he loved *me* so much." Through his death and resurrection, Jesus offers us a personal relationship with himself. That personal sacrifice demands a personal response from us. Let us respond to God by saying, "Yes, I am your daughter and you are my Father, and I want to give my whole life to you as your Son Jesus gave his to me."

The Father offers Jesus as a model for our lives. In him, we can see the way to the Father and the way to make our lives pleasing to the Father. Jesus himself sought time to be with his Father—to be renewed in power—so that he could serve him fully. In order to enter into that personal, living relationship with our Father, we need to spend time with him daily. No relationship can grow and flourish without regular, uninterrupted time to communicate. We need to come to the Father, to sit at his feet, to worship and adore him for who he is. We need to tell him about our cares and concerns. We also need to learn how to be quiet before him, to let him communicate his love and his concerns to us.

Feeling Close to God

What does it mean to "hear" the Lord? Sometimes we may sense strongly that the Lord is "saying" something to us, that he is leading us in a particular direction, while at other times we may hear him speak to us through scripture or through another person. Some days his love is just present, and we know without a doubt that he is with us. But there are other days, when our time with the Lord seems dry and unfruitful. We should never yield to the temptation to believe that God is far from us. Our emotions may make us feel close or far away from God, but he does not change and is not capricious in his love for us. Unlike human beings, God is the same today as he was yesterday and will be tomorrow. Our emotions change but his faithfulness remains the same. We need to constantly remind ourselves that our relationship with God rests on his faithful love, not on how *we* are feeling at the moment.

Too Busy to Pray

Now as they went on their way, he entered a village; and a woman named Martha received him into her house. And she had a sister called Mary, who sat at the Lord's feet and listened to his teaching. But Martha was distracted with much serving; and she went to him and said, "Lord, do you not care that my sister has left me to serve alone? Tell her then to help me." But the Lord answered her, "Martha, Martha, you are anxious and troubled about many things; one thing is needful. Mary has chosen the good portion, which shall not be taken away from her." (Lk 10:38-42)

We need to be like Mary, knowing when to take time out from our busy lives to be alone with God. Our prayertime is often the first thing that gets bumped when busyness invades our lives. If we wait until nothing extraordinary is going on, we will wind up with a very erratic prayer life, at best. We have to master our time in order to make sure that the things we deem important actually do happen. If we let circumstances rule our lives, the chances are good that our time with the Lord will be replaced by other things.

It's important to decide on a definite time each day to put

aside for the Lord. Once you've decided on one, stick to it. If the only time that is not subject to interruption is early morning, get up a half hour early. The Lord is the pearl of great price; he is worth everything we have (Mt 13:46). If the only time the house is quiet is when the baby is taking a nap, resist the urge to do the dishes and straighten the living room before coming before the Lord. If you keep your priorities straight, the other things in your life will fall into place peacefully.

Faith: A Vital Ingredient

Confident expectation in prayer offers power that no Christian can afford to live without. As we meet difficulties in our lives, we need to know that God both hears our prayers and answers them. The Lord does not listen grudgingly to our petitions. Scripture tells us that he encourages us to ask for his help. "Truly, truly, I say to you, if you ask anything of the Father, he will give it to you in my name. Hitherto you have asked nothing in my name; ask, and you will receive, that your joy may be full" (Jn 16:23-24).

Part of our relationship with the Father involves our right to ask him for the things we need. He knows better than we do how needy we really are. We can come before him in honesty and simplicity, knowing that he is a Father who has even numbered the hair of our heads.

The Lord cares about our emotional life. His concern for us is not just "spiritual." After all, he made our bodies and our emotions. We can have confidence that we will see his power at work in our emotions as well as in other areas of our lives. We can pray confidently, "Lord, show me the way out of the darkness of this depression." "Father in heaven, I know you love me, help me control my anger. It's so hard for me."

Inner Healing

Another form of prayer, one which has been very effective for many Christians, is called "healing of memories" or "inner healing." In this kind of prayer an older brother or sister in the Lord who has particular gifts of discernment and prayer asks the Lord to heal the causes of both specific and general difficulties in our lives. Certain problems may have resulted from traumatic events in our childhood, harmful past relationships, or just some unknown cause that has left us unable to experience the fullness of God's life and joy.

For example, a person who never received the right kind of love and security as a child may become an anxious and insecure adult. Humanly speaking, it's impossible to *undo* the past, to alter the effects of what has already occurred. But through specifically directed prayer for emotional healing, an anxious and insecure Christian can experience freedom from this long-term emotional bondage. Inner healing isn't the answer for every problem in life, but it can be a useful and successful tool. God has given it to us, as a gift, for our emotional and spiritual well-being.

Spiritual Warfare

"Put on the armor of God so that you may be able to stand firm against the tactics of the Devil. Our battle is not against human forces but against the principalities and powers, the rulers of this world of darkness, the evil spirit in regions above" (Eph 6:10-12).

The Christian cannot afford to be naive about the work of evil spirits, to ignore the existence of evil spiritual forces. Scripture testifies time and again that there is a force of evil working in direct opposition to the plan of God. From the story of creation to Christ's temptation in the wilderness, the evil fallen angel has worked relentlessly against God's purpose in the world.

What is the booty in the cosmic battle between God and Satan? Nothing less than the human race. We know who wins; but on the day-to-day level we are still harassed and influenced by the work of darkness in the world around us. Even so, we are not helpless victims of spiritual forces that are stronger than we are. The Holy Spirit within us is more powerful than any other spirit. We have authority over any work of darkness, not through our own virtue or power, but through the power and authority of Jesus Christ.

When we are being harassed by Satan and his evil minions, we are often tempted to forget the truth. But the truth is an essential weapon for waging battle against our enemy. Consider Jesus' example. When he was in the desert prior to his public ministry, Jesus was tempted by the evil one (see Mt 4:1-11; Lk 4:1-13). Instead of forgetting the truth, Jesus used scripture as a powerful weapon to resist temptation. He defeated every taunt of the evil one by the power of the word of God. This glimpse of the spiritual realities is both sobering and instructive—sobering because Satan dared to tempt Jesus and instructive because it illustrates the importance of having a ready and thorough knowledge of scripture.

Our minds and emotions are fair game for the evil one. He is called the accuser of the brethren (Rv 12:10) and the father of lies (Jn 8:44). What fitting names for one who constantly tries to undermine the word of God! We often expend tremendous energy trying to deal with specific problems, such as critical thoughts, anger, resentment, and guilt with little success. When evil spirits are at work, tempting, tormenting, and accusing us, self-discipline and repentance do little to alleviate the problem. However, when we combine spiritual warfare with self-discipline and repentance we can begin to make great progress.

But how do we do battle with Satan? We simply stand on the authority of Jesus and of scripture, commanding any evil spirits at work against us or against a situation to be gone. A simple prayer, such as "In the name of Jesus Christ, by the power of his death on the cross, I command any evil spirits who are harassing me to be gone right now," covers any number of situations.

Consider Barbara's experience. All week she had been serving God faithfully, loving her husband and caring for the children. Yet Thursday came and she began to be barraged with negative thoughts about herself. As she was vacuuming the living room the thought came to her, "No one really cares about me; I'm no good." As she was driving to the store that afternoon, she kept thinking, "I can't do anything right; I'm a failure." As she was doing the dinner dishes, she began to construct a mental checklist of all her faults. Then she stopped short. "Wait a minute, what's going on here," she thought. "I don't really think that I'm all that bad. Lots of people do care about me. Where are all these thoughts coming from?"

Barbara decided to take spiritual authority over these negative thoughts. "In the name of Jesus, who has all power in heaven and on earth, I command you, Satan, to stop bothering me." Later that evening she realized that self-depreciating and destructive thoughts no longer plagued her. Her usual cheerful and confident disposition had returned.

Not all negative thoughts and poor self-esteem are directly influenced by evil spirits. But we should take advantage of every part of the armor that God has so generously put at our disposal.

It isn't necessary to understand exactly how or why evil spirits operate in our lives. Too active a curiosity will center our attention on the evil one and his works, rather than on Jesus and his works. But every Christian should realize that the kingdom of light and the kingdom of darkness war against each other. Whether we like it or not, we are going to experience the effects of that war in our own lives. Fortunately for us, we can be confident that we have power and authority from God to resist and rebuke any work of darkness.

The Holy Spirit

And I will pray the Father, and he will give you another Counselor, to be with you for ever, even the Spirit of truth, whom the world cannot receive, because it neither sees him nor knows him; you know him, for he dwells with you, and will be in you. . . . But the Counselor, the Holy Spirit, whom the Father will send in my name, he will teach you all things, and bring to your remembrance all that I have said to you (Jn 14:16-17, 25-26).

When the Spirit of truth comes, he will guide you into all the truth; for he will not speak on his own authority, but whatever he hears he will speak and he will declare to you the things that are to come (Jn 16:13).

God's greatest gift to us is his Holy Spirit. His love for us is boundless. He sent his Son to save us through his death on the cross, and he gave us his Holy Spirit to help, counsel, teach, and strengthen us in our daily life.

To be a disciple of Jesus requires more than just determination and conviction. We need the kind of power that the first apostles had. The Holy Spirit empowered them to proclaim the good news of the kingdom of God boldly and fearlessly. What a contrast they must have presented to the timid, fearful apostles that hid from the Jews after Jesus' death! (See Acts 2-4; 2 Tm 1-6). Obviously, the Holy Spirit had the power to transform men and women, bound by fear and insecurity, into bold, faith-filled people who proclaimed the gospel (see Acts 2).

As Christians we can't do without that kind of supernatural help in our lives. Without it, we will be constantly frustrated in our attempts to overcome the effects of habit, powerlessness, and discouragement in dealing with our emotions.

We need to ask the Lord directly for a full release of the Holy Spirit in our own lives, to empower, strengthen, and teach us. We can expect that God will be faithful, that he will bless us as he did the apostles. For he has promised to give his Spirit to all who ask.

Be Reconciled

God has given us another beautiful gift: the power of repentance and reconciliation. The Father sent Jesus, his beloved Son, to reconcile mankind to himself. Jesus' death on the cross enables us to come home to the Father in a way that was impossible before. He was the perfect sacrifice that atoned for our sins. We now have access to the Father, *even while we are still sinners.*

One of my favorite parables is the story of the prodigal son (Lk 15:11-32). I like to think of the father's superhuman ability to forgive and love his son *despite* the wrongs he had done in the past. The parable speaks eloquently of our heavenly Father's capacity to love and forgive us. What an encouragement to anyone who struggles with thoughts like "Have I sinned once too often?" or "This sin is too big to be forgiven."

We should seek to emulate the Lord's example of forgiveness in our relationships with others. Jesus commissions us to love and forgive others as he has forgiven us (see Lk 11:2-4, 17:3-4). His exhortation to "leave your gifts at the altar and go; first be reconciled to your brother" (Mt 5:24) is a spiritual principle for our health and well-being, as well as for our spiritual growth. In the third chapter of Colossians, Paul outlines specific attitudes and actions that should characterize the Christian in a right relationship with God and others. "Bear with one another; forgive whatever grievances you have against one another" (3:13).

If reconciliation is not functioning properly in a Christian's life, the signs will be obvious. Anger, resentment, bitterness, hostility, depression, and guilt are just some of them.

The Armor of God

Therefore take the whole armor of God, that you may be able to withstand in the evil day, and having done all, to stand. Stand, therefore, having girded your loins with truth, and having put on the breastplate of righteousness, and having shod your feet with the equipment of the gospel of peace; besides all these taking the shield of faith, with which you can quench all the flaming darts of the evil one. And take the helmet of salvation, and the sword of the Spirit, which is the word of God. (Eph 6:13-17)

We are to take Paul's exhortation seriously. The armor of God is meant to equip the saints (that's us!) to live effective and holy lives until they are united forever with the Lord.

If we decide to do without one or two pieces of this armor, because they seem unattractive to us, we will face the world without the full protection God intends us to have. We would be like someone who goes out into a snowstorm without a coat. Would we have much sympathy when they cry out, "Save me from this terrible storm?" Often we get into trouble because of our own negligence; we find ourselves facing life without the full protection that God intended.

The Power of Scripture to Transform Us

"All scripture is inspired by God and profitable for teaching, for reproof, for correction, and for training in righteousness, that the man [or woman!] of God may be complete, equipped for every good work" (2 Tm 3:16-17).

If we want to know the mind of God, to know how to act, think, and relate as the Lord intends, we need to *know the truth*. We need to be able to hold on to a word from scripture that strengthens us when we are weak, tempted, or confused.

Scripture says to "stand fast, with the truth as the belt around your waist" (Eph 6:14). The fully equipped Christian lives not on the defensive but on the offensive. Such a Christian is a strength for God's kingdom. She remembers that "everything written before our time was written for our instruction, that we might derive hope from the lessons of patience and the words of encouragement of the Scriptures" (Rom 15:4).

Righteous Living: A Key to Emotional Health

The breastplate of righteousness is essential apparel for the "well-dressed" Christian. One way to stay healthy spiritually, emotionally, and physically is to follow the way of the Lord. Of course, this is not to say that a person who is physically or emotionally ill has necessarily become so because of some sin they have committed. But those who walk in the way of the Lord, who keep his commands, who live a righteous life, do enjoy the fruit of that walk. In fact, some of our problems stem from past or from present wrongdoing. Past immorality, wrong relating, selfishness, and other sins take a toll on us emotionally and spiritually. We can avoid some of our emotional problems by behaving and thinking in Christlike ways.

Christian Fellowship

Another important element of our lives as Christians has to do with the brothers and sisters the Lord gives to us. Many Christians behave as though God is the only person they need. And in one sense that's true. But one of the ways we come to know the love, support, and encouragement that he wants to give us is through other Christian men and women.

The epistles were written to groups of Christians, to churches that were living Christian communities. The writers of the epistles were addressing Christians who knew the meaning of real brotherhood, of common commitment to the Lord and to each other. Of course the churches differed from each other in their organization. Some held everything in common (see Acts 2:44-47), while others didn't live together but gathered for prayer and fellowship regularly. Nevertheless, scripture and Christian tradition indicate that the Christian life was never intended to be lived alone. Unfortunately, few churches today display evidence of this love and intimate sharing of faith in Jesus. The level of fellowship is often congenial but superficial. And there is little sign of the power that should accompany God's people when they gather together. Let us remember this exhortation: "Beloved, if God so loved us, we also ought to love one another. No man has ever seen God; if we love one another, God abides in us and his love is perfected in us" (1 Jn 4:11-12).

In a world where many profess a kind of "cultural Christianity," it is important to seek out other men and women who have accepted Jesus as their Lord, and who have made a conscious decision to live a radical Christian life. One good way to find them is to check your local church bulletin, which may advertise prayer groups or Bible studies. If you're serious about finding regular Christian fellowship, it is usually worth investigating these groups. The fellowship of other committed Christians can provide you with much that is necessary to live the Christian life with power.

Why Is Christian Fellowship So Important?

Prayer. When Christians gather together their prayer can have great power. "Again I say to you, if two of you agree on earth about anything they ask, it will be done for them by my Father in heaven. For where two or three are gathered in my name there am I in the midst of them" (Mt 18:19-20).

Wisdom. When Christians gather there is a greater pool of wisdom and experience to draw from. We need the help of others to keep us on the right path, maturing as sons and daughters of God.

Support. As disciples of Christ, it helps to know that there are others who desire the same life. If we are feeling that we have little energy to continue fighting the "good fight," a brother or sister can encourage us to stir up the love of God within us. Their faithfulness can help us to persevere.

Service. Christian commitment gives birth to a desire to serve. Often, within the context of a prayer group or Bible study we can live out that desire by loving and serving God's people together. By doing so, we will be imitating Christ, the servant par excellence.

Two Strengths Working Together

The basis for a healthy emotional and spiritual life is found in a strong relationship with the Lord and in fellowship with other Christians. Prayer and scripture nourish and give growth to our ever-maturing relationship with God the Father and his Son Jesus Christ. As we grow in our knowledge of God, we will be able to come before him more confidently any time of the day or night. We will have confidence as a daughter of the King, a daughter who has access to his throne room and who is welcomed with open arms by her Father.

The Holy Spirit empowers us to love others and to live the life of a disciple of Jesus. The Spirit equips us to worship the Father by giving us gifts (see 1 Cor 11-13). We can ask Jesus to release the power of the Holy Spirit and the fullness of his gifts in us. The Lord intends to equip us with everything we need to live a holy and righteous life.

Gratefully we receive the strength and support provided by the fellowship of other Christians in our lives. We can pray together, share together, and learn together as we come before our Father as his family. If we ask the Lord to give us other Christians with whom to share our lives, he will provide.

As we consider specific difficulties in our emotional lives, we can face them with the confidence that comes from living a faith-filled life, centered on Jesus and consistent with the teaching of scripture. As we do so, we will experience a freedom and strength that we may have thought beyond our grasp.

Come, Holy Spirit, and teach me the ways of God. Train me to use the spiritual tools that you have given me so that I may walk in confidence with my Lord. And may Jesus Christ be the one true cornerstone of my life.

THREE

The Mind— Gateway to Our Emotions

FOR THE GREATER PART of my life, I don't think I ever sufficiently reflected on what did or did not affect my emotions. They were simply part of me, to be enjoyed, tolerated, or controlled, depending on the situation. However, about six years ago I began meeting with a group of Christian women to talk about our emotional lives so we could begin to understand God's plan more fully. After several discussions, it became startlingly clear to us that no matter how different we were in personality, emotional makeup, or background, a strong and very direct connection existed within each of us between our emotions and our minds.

Let me share some examples to illustrate the powerful effect that our thoughts can have on our emotions and vice versa.

Carol, 26 and newly married, was not a very organized person. However, her husband John was a meticulous man who valued efficiency and accuracy. Carol related this incident:

One afternoon I came home from teaching nursery school, had a snack, and decided to sit down and enjoy a well-deserved break before starting supper. I picked up a weekly news magazine and continued to read it long after I knew I should have been up and preparing supper. In the back of my mind I was beginning to feel guilty about reading so long and making dinner late. Immediately I began to prepare a defense for myself so that I could anticipate John's questions about why dinner was late. A conversation developed in my mind while I was dashing about the kitchen. What would John say and how would I respond? By the time he did come home for dinner I had already been arguing with him in my mind for the last forty-five minutes. I was so angry with him about our imaginary conversation that I wasn't speaking to him when he did walk in the door.

It's easy to see that Carol's thought patterns directly affected her emotions. What began as a few twinges of guilt gave birth to all-out anger, in spite of the fact that nothing had actually happened between John and herself. She would have done better to face up to the facts: she spent too much time reading when she should have been preparing dinner. Instead, she chose to deal with her guilt by becoming defensive and angry. Her view of the situation had become distorted, until it bore little resemblance to what had actually happened. Her emotional intensity was divorced from the reality of the situation. It ended up having a substantial effect on their relationship.

When John came home from work and didn't say anything about dinner being late, I said to myself, "Oh good, off the hook!" But later on that evening, when John and I began to talk about some small thing that was not working right in another area of our life together, I got very, very angry with him. And it took three days for us to sort out this big mess.

Carol had dwelt on all the things John might say about dinner being late. She had stored up an arsenal of anger, which exploded later when they were trying to deal with a relatively insignificant problem. Her thoughts had generated a new problem, which had to be worked out at the expense of them both.

Another good example comes from Betty, a single woman of forty with a secretarial job that suited her talents and financial needs well. Betty tended to be overly sensitive to what people, especially those with more prestigious jobs, thought of her. Even the smallest slight would affect her deeply. At the prayer meeting she attended she was entrusted with the service of selling books. She handled the job well and was a good steward of the books and the finances. One week the prayer meeting leader told her that another woman would begin helping her since such long lines had developed every week at the book table.

Betty thought the decision was fine, and she genuinely appreciated the help. But the next morning at work she found herself pounding her typewriter mercilessly. Her mind was troubled. It had begun with a quiet and seemingly reasonable train of thought: "I wonder what the new woman will be like to work with. I wonder why the leader all of a sudden thought I needed help. Maybe I'm not doing a good job. Maybe this woman will do it better; they may want her to replace me eventually. They probably didn't want to hurt me and are trying to ease me out gently. I know that I've never gone to college, but my accounts always balance at the end of the month." And so her thoughts would lead her.

By the following week, Betty was depressed and had difficulty coping with her work at the office. She found herself crying in the women's bathroom. Maybe she should quit her job. She didn't seem to be able to do anything right. When she went to the prayer meeting that Thursday evening, there wasn't much joy in her heart.

Betty had accepted the leader's direction regarding her service. At first, she even thought it was a good idea. But then she began to imagine other motives for the change, and her thoughts began to affect not only her service at the book table, but her relationship with the Lord and with others. Her thoughts began to eat away at her confidence and self-esteem until she became depressed.

The link between our thoughts and our emotions is clear enough in these examples. Are we forever prey to our emotions and our thoughts? How can we control them without repressing them?

A Reasonable Alternative

Scripture tells us that it is not only possible but necessary to be in charge of our thought life if we are to live the Christian life. "I appeal to you therefore, brethren, by the mercies of God, to present your bodies as a living sacrifice, holy and acceptable to God, which is your spiritual worship. Do not be conformed to this world but be transformed by the renewal of your mind, that you may prove what is the will of God, what is good and acceptable and perfect" (Rom 12:1-2).

You—your body and mind—are the spiritual worship which is pleasing to God. It is not just your words that praise God but what is in your minds and heart. The *unrenewed* mind cannot discern the will of God—what is good, acceptable, and perfect. In other words, unless your mind is submitted to God's order, you will be severely handicapped when it comes to living the Christian life.

For most of us, it is true to say that our minds have been formed by the world, not by the will of God. One day's evaluation of our thought life will probably be enough to convince us that a mighty work of renewal and transformation needs to occur in our minds if we are to truly live the Christian life. We cannot straddle the fence, with one foot in the kingdom of God and the other in the world. Sooner or later we will need to take our stand in one place or the other.

A Renewed Mind

What does the renewed mind that Paul talks about in Romans look like? What is the goal toward which we are working? "Finally, brethren, whatever is true, whatever is honorable, whatever is just, whatever is pure, whatever is lovely, whatever is gracious, if there is any excellence, if there is anything worthy of praise, think about these things. What you have learned and received and heard and seen in me, do; and the God of peace will be with you" (Phil 4:8-9).

A renewed mind is one that obeys our will and the will of God. It hasn't got an independent will, but is ready to be directed and contained as we desire. The renewed mind has Jesus Christ as its master and is in harmony with the will of the Father. The things that occupy our minds and our individual thoughts should reflect and support our Christian commitment. We need to be prepared to spend time and energy to mold and form our minds according to Jesus' mind. Anything so crucial to our Christian life is well worth the effort.

Consider Paul's directions to the Philippians. "Have no anxiety about anything, but in everything by prayer and supplication with thanksgiving let your requests be made known to God" (Phil 4:6). Paul offers us sound guidelines, stating clearly the areas with which the renewed mind should occupy itself. Of course we can't ignore all the necessary and practical details of our lives. But we can make sure that we approach even the smallest practical detail with an attitude of love and service. As we put away malice, wrath, slander, and judgment, our attitudes toward our families and toward others the Lord has given us to love will change radically. Our burden of self-concern and self-pity will fade into the background as we focus on the Lord and on loving and serving his people.

Does this sound like an unreachable goal? Believe me, it's not. Don't say to yourself, "I can't do that; it would take a saint to accomplish that." Other women like ourselves have won the victory over their thought lives and we can too. Just because their minds are renewed minds doesn't mean that they never struggle with temptation or yield to sin. But it does mean that they have *decided* to have a renewed mind. They began by asking the Lord for his help and grace to overcome habitual thought patterns. Through the grace of God, the love of Jesus Christ, the witness of scripture, and the strength that comes from personal discipline, many women have been able to gain control of their thought life so that it can be put to the service of God.

How do we begin to do this? First, we should understand that our thought life is not independent of the rest of our personality. It is an integral part of us. If it is to serve our Christian life rather than dictate to us, we need to be able to control it properly.

Who's in Charge?

Here is a little test you can take to find out who's in charge—
you or your mind.

1. Can you account for what goes on in your mind during the
day? While no one can account for sixteen hours of every
waking day, nevertheless it can be extremely enlightening to try
to remember what you thought about while waiting for a bus,
talking on the phone to a long-winded friend, waiting in line for
gas, or folding the laundry. Did you choose to think each of
those thoughts, or did you just "interrupt" a conversation that
was already being carried on in your head?

2. Once you get in touch with some of your thoughts, do you
like what you find? Or do you find that you are often critical of
others? Does your mind conduct an ongoing analysis of the
problems and faults of others? Is it filled with frantic thoughts
about what might happen if your child is kidnapped, you lose
your job, you aren't able to make ends meet, a man breaks into
the house when you're alone? Is it filled with self-concern—
with thoughts of me, me, me?

3. Are you building a fantasy life in order to escape present
frustration or pain? Are the situations you reflect on real? Are
the relationships real? Are the conversations real?

4. Is your mind overactive? Is it always buzzing with
thoughts about this or that, flitting from one thing to another?
Are you successful when you try to stop a train or pattern of
thought? Does your mind do what you want, or does it fight for
what *it* wants to think? Does your mind continually return to a
train of thought from which you are trying to divert it?

If you recognize any, some, or all of these typical states of
mind, then it's time to take account of your thoughts and the
fruit they bear. If you avoid making a decision to retrain your
mind, your emotions will only continue to cause frustration and
discouragement.

Let's examine the points raised in these four areas in order to
understand what we're dealing with and what steps we need to
take in order to change.

Discipline and Faith in God

If you've ever had dogs, you know that there's a big difference between one that is well-trained and one that pays no attention to his master's commands. A friend of ours once bought a lovable little puppy for his children. But it grew up to become a large, unmanageable dog. No one had succeeded in training the dog to come when it was called or to sit still or to heel. Instead, it bolted out of the kennel every time one of the children came to feed it and took off to the nearby park to frolic. The following forty-five minutes were spent chasing, calling, cajoling, threatening, and pleading with the dog to come. All the time the dog would cavort about, sometimes racing just within reach and then bolting merrily away. That lovable dog had become a source of frustration instead of a joy to the family.

Our minds can behave in a similar way if they have never been made to submit to our will. When we want to stop thinking critically of someone, we commonly find that our minds refuse to obey. When we want to stop some sexual fantasy, to call "heel" to our minds, they may stray back to the same thoughts consistently. When we try to sleep at night, our minds may race from one anxious thought to another.

The first thing we need to do is to believe that things can change, that we are not saddled with this problem forever. Naturally, we can change things to some extent through sheer determination and willpower. But as Christians, we must first be able to rely on the power of the Holy Spirit to help us in our weakness. We can be certain that our thought life is important to God and that he wants it to be in good order even more than we do. And he doesn't require us to accomplish this on our own. Remember, God has given us the power of his Spirit and the inspiring example of the saints who have gone before us to help us in our struggle.

Next, we need to identify one or two specific periods of time during the day when our thoughts are particularly prone to wander. We can make a special effort during these times to discipline our minds. Deciding to attack everything at once will only overwhelm and discourage us.

We also need to have on hand specific thoughts to substitute for the unwanted ones. For example, if we are habitually anxious, we should decide to replace each anxious thought with some specific thought about the Lord's faithfulness to us. Then we can praise him for it.

One woman, Gloria, knew that she had difficulty controlling her thoughts. She found it particularly hard to stop thinking critically about other people. She knew that her thoughts affected her ability to love and care for others. She also knew that the problem was more pronounced when she was performing repetitive tasks, like folding laundry, waiting in line at the grocery store, or driving the car. These were the times that she would be most likely to think about other people's faults. To deal with the problem, she began by asking the Lord for strength to redirect her thoughts. She also decided to pay particular attention to what she thought about while driving the car. She would to call to mind at least one good quality about the person in question. Then she would pray for a list of intentions, which she carried with her in the car, in order to redirect her thoughts to the Lord and to good.

The first evening she felt like a total failure. Every time she caught herself analyzing others, she would stop. But moments later she would begin to think the same negative thoughts. After several weeks of this daily discipline, she noticed that it had become more natural for her to pray for others when their faults came to mind. She also found that she was getting better at recognizing and halting judgmental thoughts when they occurred at other times during the day. Victory didn't come overnight. It took months of consistent and faithful effort. But eventually Gloria was able to redirect the routes her mind took when it was not specifically occupied.

Most of us have difficulty following Paul's instruction to bring every thought captive to Christ (2 Cor 10:4-5). And it's no wonder. After a heavy spring rain, water rushes down the paths that offer the least resistance. If a rock or bunch of sticks obstruct its course, it simply flows around them. Our minds operate in a similar way. Our thoughts run along the most comfortable and familiar pathways. It takes firm resolve to redirect them onto new routes.

Stopping Your Thoughts Immediately

A key to this retraining process is to nip the unwanted thought in the bud. We are often deceived into thinking that the early stages of a thought pattern are harmless. But if we wait until a thought is obviously sinful or wrong, it's usually almost impossible to stop it. It has become too big, too familiar, or too powerful to be dealt with easily.

To be able to stop unwanted thought patterns, you need to know yourself and the way you work. If you are prone to anxiety, you need to recognize the thought patterns that act as early warning signs of anxiety. A thought like "I sure hope the kids don't get chicken pox on vacation" could lead to increased anxiety about the children and your vacation. Stop at once and choose to think positively. Then thank the Lord for the way he loves and cares for you.

It's easy for us to excuse our lack of mental discipline, especially when we take pleasure in our thoughts. Although anxiety does not "feel" good, it can bring a form of pleasure. Worrying can make us feel that we are being responsible—a good mother is supposed to worry, isn't she? So our anxiety is reinforced by our need to feel responsible.

But with God's power and our willingness to learn self-discipline, we, like Gloria, can do what God's word calls us to do: "For though we live in the world we are not carrying on a worldly war, for the weapons of our warfare are not worldly but have divine power to destroy strongholds. We destroy arguments and every proud obstacle to the knowledge of God, and take every thought captive to obey Christ" (2 Cor 10:4-5).

Mental self-discipline is essential if we are to overcome such worldly thoughts as anxiety, sexual fantasy, preoccupation with material possessions, self-pity, and self-concern. In summary, we need to ask for the *grace of God*, choose a *realistic goal* at the start, and have specific *substitute thoughts* to replace the unwanted ones. "Finally, brethren, whatever is true, whatever is honorable, whatever is just, whatever is pure, whatever is lovely, whatever is gracious, if there is anything worthy of praise, think about these things" (Phil 4:8).

We are to persevere, to fight the good fight, remembering that freedom is the prize. It is well worth the energy and the time we invest to win it. We should remember the promise in Romans, "Do not be conformed to this world but be transformed by the renewal of your mind, that you may prove what is the will of God, what is good and acceptable and perfect" (12:2). Let's take Paul's words to the Philippians to heart: "Have no anxiety about anything, but in everything by prayer and supplication with thanksgiving let your requests be made known to God. And the peace of God, which passes all understanding, will keep your hearts and your minds in Christ Jesus" (4:6-7).

The Evil One

The problem with our minds cannot be solved by self-discipline alone, because our minds are the battleground on which many forces contend for control. Old thought habits, the pressing practical cares of the day, the Lord himself, and the evil one are rivals for the "air time" of our minds. We can't forget that we live in a spiritual as well as a physical world.

Since we are one with Christ, we have not only entered into salvation, but we have also entered into a spiritual battle between God and Satan that began in heaven. Though Jesus Christ has won the ultimate victory through his death and resurrection, the evil one continues to war against us. He does his best to prevent us from being the holy women the Lord wants us to be. Much of his work is directed against our minds. If Satan can plant doubts, fears, anxieties, and sinful thoughts and desires in us, he can wear down our spiritual and emotional energies, making us more vulnerable to attack. We should not discount his activity but should guard our minds against him.

But how can we recognize the voice of the evil one? We can begin by asking ourselves: "Would the Lord himself think this or want me to think this?" Scripture is our guideline for answering this question. For example, suppose a thought is making us fearful. We know that scripture encourages us to fear nothing, because our Father in heaven knows our needs and will take care of us (see Lk 12:22-31). Or perhaps we are entertaining thoughts of ill will toward a person we love. It's clear that such thoughts contradict God's word and our fundamental desire to love. Even if we are unsure that the thought was planted by the evil one, it's better to take spiritual authority over it, to command the evil one to leave, than to err in the direction of discounting his influence on our thought life. No harm is done if we command him to leave us alone. But if we ignore his influence in our lives, we are bound to struggle needlessly and ineffectively with uncontrollable thoughts which come from him. A simple command in the name of Jesus is all that is needed. "In the name of Jesus Christ I command you, Satan, to leave my thoughts alone."

After taking spiritual authority, we must then apply the faith and discipline essential for bringing our unruly thoughts under control. Faith, discipline, and spiritual authority are a powerful combination for bringing every thought captive to Christ.

Imagination and Fantasy

Another major area of our thought life is fantasy. If we want to have better control over our thought life, we have to understand how our imagination works; and it's essential that it work in the right way, since it has the capacity either to help or hinder our efforts to live the Christian life. The Lord gave us the gift of our imagination to help us love and serve him and his people creatively, according to the individual gifts and abilities that we each have. It's good, for instance, to imagine how the Lord must be; we can enhance our understanding of the psalms and other parts of scripture by picturing the love, mercy, and justice of God. Sometimes, picturing in our minds the correct

way to act in different situations helps us behave righteously.
We ought to use our imagination only in a way that directly
contributes to our love of God and of one another. It is clearly
wrong to use it in a way that is sinful and or that leads to sinful
actions. And it is also wrong to use our imagination in ways that
seem harmless but that do not actually contribute to our ability
to love and serve God and others. It's essential to keep this
guideline in mind, for scripture is very direct about how
Christians ought to think and behave.

A common form of fantasy among women is daydreaming.
Our minds drift unconsciously to conversations, relationships,
or situations, and our thoughts about them can either produce
pleasurable images which substitute for the immediate reality,
or negative images which instill fear, anxiety, anger, or hostility.
Women often fantasize about a better life than the one which
they currently experience. A woman may imagine a different
lifestyle, one that holds more excitement and adventure than
her own, or a job that utilizes all the real or imagined talent
which is being overlooked at the moment. She may fantasize
about receiving acclaim from co-workers and neighbors or
about having an affair with an attractive, exciting man who
treats her better and excites her more than the man she is
presently dating. Sometimes the fantasy includes real people,
such as her boss, or a friend's husband, or it may involve a tragic
occurence which in some way fulfills the fantasy.

This is not an appropriate way to occupy ourselves as
Christian women, for several reasons. Fantasy is a form of
escape from the immediate realities of daily life. The Lord
wants us to handle the tediousness and hardships of life by
relying on him for strength and joy to live the Christian life. But
what about those of us whose lives have been especially
difficult, perhaps because of an abusive or unresponsive
husband, divorce, personal tragedy, financial hardship, or the
death of someone close to us? Paul writes to the Corinthians,
"No temptation has overtaken you that is not common to man.
God is faithful, and he will not let you be tempted beyond your
strength, but with the temptation will also provide the way of

escape, that you may be able to endure it" (1 Cor 10:13). Scripture refers unceasingly to the faithfulness of God, his love, mercy, and provision for those who love him. Instead of escaping through fantasy, let us turn to the Lord and search the scriptures, filling our minds with the promises of God.

Fantasy Is Habit-Forming

Fantasy offers us another opportunity to apply the discipline and faith needed to control our thoughts. We need to entrust our lives and well-being into the hands of the Lord of Lords and the King of Kings. Sarah, the wife of Abraham, stands as a good model for faith in God. "By faith Sarah herself received power to conceive, even when she was past the age, since she considered *him faithful who had promised*" (Heb 11:11).

Though originally under our control, fantasy can soon become the master of our waking time. The more we give our minds over to it the more vivid it will become. Fantasy is a preoccupation that usurps the place of real people and real situations; it quickly becomes an obstacle to receiving the grace and the gift of God in our lives. We may become unable to recognize God's provision for us because it may not match the details that we have woven through our fantasy. It is easy for fantasized solutions to our problems to take on grand proportions, overshadowing the gifts of God.

It is also self-defeating to allow our imagination to stir up fear and anxiety or to generate bad feelings toward others. Sometimes daydreaming can lead to thoughts like "What if I get cancer?"; "What if I never get married?"; "What if I lose my job?" Our minds become full of gruesome details as we imagine the pain, loneliness, and anxiety we might experience. These kinds of thoughts only give birth to more anxiety, fear, and loneliness. They are part of a vicious cycle that provides no relief. It usually never helps to imagine difficult things; it never constructively prepares us for their actual occurrence. Such thinking only bears bad fruit, a sign that this way of using our imagination is not from the Lord. The Spirit of

God doesn't prompt this train of thought.

More will be said about the role of the mind and imagination in controlling anxiety and fear in later chapters dealing specifically with these emotions.

The Influence of the Media

The media has a tremendous effect on our thought life. Television shows, advertisements, magazines, music, and books inundate us daily with a torrent of impressions, information, and opinions, with which Christians of other centuries never had to contend. Most of what we are exposed to through these sources contradicts or ignores the ideal of life presented to us in scripture. Television is full of the kind of humor that tears people down and mocks their integrity as human beings. Immoral relationships have come to be the focal point of situation comedies. Characters in soap operas live bizarre lives and stand as examples of people who let their emotions rule them. Magazines and unrealistic romantic novelettes often give advice on how to attract men, have a lover without your husband knowing it, find an inexpensive abortionist, or steal someone else's job.

Advertisements often exalt material possessions as the goal every healthy American woman should spend her life pursuing. The middle- or upper-class ideal has become the pearl of great price, which people are careening deeper and deeper into debt to obtain. The promoter tries to convince the consumer that she would be much happier and more fulfilled if only she would purchase their product. On an intellectual level, she may understand what the promoter is doing. But on another level, a seed has been planted that will take root and grow. That seed is dissatisfaction, and it will try to convince her that she won't be happy until she can have, wear, look at, or exhibit the promoter's product. Such promotion is skillfully conducted. Advertising agencies spend tremendous amounts of time and money to research the most effective way to sell their products. Of course the ad agencies don't take responsibility for the dissatisfaction and depression that may come if one's life does not measure up to their latest set of standards. Christians need to take that responsibility themselves by deciding just how much of the media they will expose themselves to.

Statistics indicate that most married couples argue about money and how to spend it. I believe that some of the problem is triggered by the media's constant barrage on a woman's senses: "Buy me and you'll be prettier, or happier, or a better wife and mother." It is a wise woman who examines herself to evaluate how the media affects her desires and her attitude toward life. If she finds that the media is feeding feelings of anxiety about herself and her popularity, then she would do well to eliminate as much of the media as possible from her daily life. If her desire for material possessions stimulates dissatisfaction and makes her mildly depressed, she should consider just how all the television commercials and advertisements in women's magazines affect and stir up that desire and discontent.

We are also affected by the music we listen to. Music can soothe, bring peace, stir up praise of God, or produce joy. Or it can communicate a number of negative emotions. For the purpose of this chapter I want to deal with only two kinds of music: rock music and popular ballads. Both have one or two major themes. They are either concerned with romance and sex or with breaking away and becoming free in some way. Songs about romantic love can either stimulate you to love the man you are engaged or married to or they can make you desire a more romantic relationship than your present one. If you are single and not dating, romantic love songs can both stimulate your desire for a sexual relationship and make you depressed because your romantic fantasy has no basis in reality. For a woman who has difficulty with masturbation or sexual desire, this kind of music only aggravates the problem.

Music whose theme is the search for freedom from commitment and responsibility can also have a profound effect on our emotional life. Not only the words to the songs but also the beat communicate so much to one's emotions. These songs can work in a subtle way to dissatisfy us. In whatever form, songs of rebellion against society and authority spread their poison to their listeners, whether the listener intellectually assents to the concepts or not. Of course, I am not saying that all popular music is harmful, but it is important to recognize the tremendous effect that music can have on our emotional life.

Years of exposure to the media's unchristian view of life, love, and happiness take a toll. None of us are so strong that we can say with assurance that the media has had no adverse effect on us. Usually the effect is a subtle one. But consider this. Most of us now find the situations that used to shock us five years ago amusing or at least tolerable. Our dissatisfaction with our income level, clothes, husband, children, job, or sex life has probably increased as well. What has been presented to us on a day-in day-out basis has, over a period of time, affected our expectations of our lives and relationships. In the end, we no longer take the Christian model of what constitutes a righteous life as our norm. Unless we wake up to the impact of the media on our lives, we will be unable to understand the source of many of our difficulties with our thoughts and emotions.

Is It Worth the Effort?

What is the fruit of all this effort? What is the prize we so diligently seek? Our hard work and effort to bring our minds under the lordship of Jesus Christ will allow us to experience the fruit of the Holy Spirit in a full way once we have trained our minds to obey us.

First, we will be able to overcome specific problems with anxiety, fear, lack of sexual control, anger, and self-pity when our thoughts are not allowed to run away on their own. Second, we will be able to distinguish the Lord's voice in our daily lives because we will have learned to recognize all the other voices begging for our attention. Third, we will be able to hear and obey the Lord when he wants us to spend time with him or when he wants to give us specific directions. We will be able to respond to him peacefully since our minds will not be plagued with anxious thoughts or fears.

Control over our thoughts will enable us to "put on then, as God's chosen ones, holy and beloved, compassion, kindness, lowliness, meekness and patience, forbearing one another and, if one has a complaint against another, forgiving each other; as the Lord has forgiven you, so you also must forgive. And above all these put on love, which binds everything together in perfect harmony" (Col 3:12-14). As a result of God's grace and our efforts, we will experience new spiritual power to live the Christian life and to live it effectively.

Lord, my thoughts sometimes run out of control. Give me your strength to become a good steward over my mind. My mind belongs to you, Lord. Form it in a way that is pleasing to you.

FOUR

Self-Esteem

Do you believe that you are precious in the sight of the Lord, that you are pleasing to him, and that he rejoices when he considers you? Do you know that you are not a mistake, someone who somehow is allowed to share redemption along with other, more worthy Christians?

Sin, weakness, failure, inadequacy (both real and imagined), insecurity, and harsh self-judgment cripple many good Christian women. If we were to take a peek into the inner workings of a sampling of women, we would find that many of them suffer from what is commonly called a poor self-image. Thoughts of "I'm ugly"; "I'm too fat"; "I'll never do that well"; "I'm no good"; "Nobody really likes me"; "I'm too clumsy to do that"; "Clothes don't look right on me"; "If I died no one would miss me" are all telltale marks of someone with an inadequate self-concept. Some women suffer from it chronically while others only wrestle periodically with such thoughts and feelings.

Whether it's a daily struggle or a weekly annoyance, the Lord wants to free us from the bondage of a poor self-image. Although negative thoughts and feelings are often directed inwards, they have far-reaching repercussions. A negative self-concept is an obstacle to our relationship with the Lord and with others. It prevents us from being who we truly are—the warm, loving servants that the Lord intends us to be.

I've used the words crippled and handicapped to describe women with a poor self-image. These are vivid and accurate words that can effectively communicate the extent of the damage incurred by a poor self-image. Living the Christian life with a negative view of oneself is like trying to run the Boston marathon with only one leg. If we are convinced that we are basically unlovable or unacceptable, we will have difficulty relating to the Lord. If we feel guilty or inferior we will probably approach the Lord in prayer more like a slave than a daughter of the King. Such feelings can make us think that the Lord merely tolerates or endures us, rather than loves and cares for us.

A negative self-image also distorts our relationships with our family, friends, and acquaintances. It affects the way we speak, act, and perceive life. It can make us overly sensitive, and this sensitivity only compounds the rejection, inadequacy, and insecurity with which we may already struggle.

Furthermore, these feelings of unattractiveness, rejection, and inadequacy generate and perpetuate other emotions. "I'm unlovable"—just two words that we may sincerely believe to be true can create feelings of sadness, rejection, anxiety, and depresssion. "I'm ugly" feeds feelings of self-hatred, depression and anger. Thus, almost before we know it, one negative thought about ourselves leads us into a confrontation with an overwhelming host of negative emotions.

Our estimation of ourselves and our relationship with God and others can all be seriously affected by a negative self-image. The Lord wants us to receive his redemptive love, his protection, mercy, and reassurance. But a poor self-image closes us off from what we need most. He also wants us to have brothers and sisters with whom we can live life in a loving, supportive way. Here again, a negative self-image can create barriers that separate us from them and their support.

Jesus Christ saved us and gave us an inheritance as daughters of the Father. We are supposed to take justifiable pride in knowing that we are his women. A poor self-image poisons and destroys the truth, until we forget who we really are. Before we can tackle problems with specific emotions, we need to achieve greater freedom and accuracy in how we see ourselves.

What Can We Do about It?

Are you ready to hear the truth? Don't be surprised if you squirm a bit when I tell you. After twenty, thirty, forty, or fifty years of seeing yourself in a particular way, it can be uncomfortable to look at yourself in an altogether different light. Let's start at the beginning.

First of all, we should consider the possibility that *the way we see ourselves just may not be a complete and truthful picture*. We develop our self-image from our experiences with our parents, teachers, childhood friends and enemies, and from our successes and failures. As we grow up these perceptions often contain a mixture of truth and lies. Our perception of who we are is not always *objectively* accurate. No matter how personally convinced of it we are, it is still a *subjective* perception. We need trustworthy, accurate, and loving feedback to tell us who we are and what we are like.

First and most importantly, let us go to our Creator. We have to admit that the Lord is more objective than we are and that the Creator knows his creature. God made not only the entire universe—the stars, planets, air, water, land, and all creatures that swim, crawl, or fly—but also man, the crown of his creative act. And man, his masterpiece, was created to bear God's own image (see Gn 1:27). "God saw everything that he had made, and behold, it was very good" (Gn 1:31).

Behold, *you* are very good. Yes, you! Unless you want to call God a liar or to say that God is imperfect, that he made a mistake when he created you, you need to reevaluate how you perceive yourself. You are not a mistake, just a biological by-product. You are unique and good, and God loves you very personally. You bear his image and likeness.

> For thou didst form my inward parts,
>> thou didst knit me together in my mother's womb.
> I praise thee, for thou art fearful and wonderful.
>> Wonderful are thy works!

Thou knowest me right well;
  my frame was not hidden from thee,
when I was being made in secret,
  intricately wrought in the depths of the earth.
Thy eyes beheld my unformed substance;
  in thy book were written, every one of them,
the days that were formed for me,
  when as yet there was none of them. (Ps 139:13-16)

Yes, God knows all about you, your strengths and your weaknesses, and yet his love and acceptance is constant. It isn't easy to understand godly love. For we suffer here on earth from fickle, ungodly love. We need to see that God's love and acceptance is real and unconditional. He is loving the *real* you, not the you that's been created in your mind. He sees you more clearly and accurately than anyone can. You are beautiful before the Lord. (Don't squirm. It's true.) And he is pleased with you.

Comparison—A Trap!

Our uniqueness, what makes each of us who we are, must be valued for itself. The physical nature, gifts, talents, and abilities God has given us have value *apart from how we compare to anyone else*. Comparison is deadly. It's one of the surest ways to undermine our self-image. It's also wrong. Measuring our looks, personality, or talents against any one else's shows disrespect for God's creation and for his own reflection in us. To say that God made one person better than another is inconsistent with what we know about God himself. Usually the problem concerns our rule of measurement. We measure ourselves and others by standards that the world esteems. Are you beautiful compared to several famous models? Probably not. Few women have the "perfect" look, and it is only "perfect" according to the standard set by the advertising agencies and movie producers. Are you well-liked? Are you popular? Again, popularity is a worldly concept, and its measurement is narrow and unspiritual. Even ability, what we can or can't do, is primarily measured by what happens to be popular and "in," or it is based on a standard of excellence that few people can ever achieve.

By the world's standards, very few of us "measure up." This concept of measuring up to some standard is a trap that is nearly impossible to get free from once we become entangled in it. It is like quicksand; the more we struggle to conform to impossible standards the deeper we become mired in our endless search for perfection. The reward for finally measuring up to these worldly standards is supposed to be perfect happiness. But what an elusive reward it proves to be! Only in Christ can we find happiness; nothing but the Lord himself can give us lasting happiness. All other forms of happiness and joy are fleeting. Of course they look pretty attractive and inviting at times. But if we keep before us the joy that comes from knowing the Lord Jesus, the world's idea of happiness can be put into the place that it deserves—last place.

Ideals and Models

During childhood, a very important process takes place in us. We form expectations about the kind of person we want to be and the kind of person other people want us to be. For myself, my mother, Dale Evans, St. Therese of Lisieux, and Superman were important models. They made that seven-year-old girl in me want to grow up to be the type of woman who loved God and did it heroically, and all the while having fun of course! Often our ideals are modelled on the lives of several influential people or sometimes formed as a reaction against other people. I was sure, for example, that I never wanted to be like the lady up the street who screamed at her kids all day. Some of these influences are healthy ones. We are meant to understand ourselves better by relating to others around us.

As we mature into adulthood, these ideals are meant to be tempered by reality. Common sense, maturity, and experience should play a decisive role in helping us adjust our childhood values to adult goals and expectations. I have come to expect that I *probably* will never fly like Superman and to realize that a cowgirl is no longer the epitome of womanhood. That change has signalled that the right process has taken place in my life. But not all my goals have changed. I still want to be the good, holy woman that God wants me to be.

Without that maturing process, our childhood ideals and models will clash with the reality of adult life, and we will suffer the consequences, particularly in our emotional life. Our expectations of the way life *should* be, the way we *should* be, and the way others *should* be will not line up with the way life really is, with our abilities, and the abilities of others. So life can often become confusing, disappointing, and frustrating.

Miriam, a woman in her late forties, first came to me several years ago about a problem she had with depression. Eventually it became clear that she was suffering from a bad case of misplaced ideals. Her mother was a perfectionist who communicated all too effectively that "good" girls *always* did *everything* right. Because Miriam was naturally gifted, she usually lived up to those standards. But whenever she did not, she would become discouraged and often depressed.

Years later she experienced a renewal of her childhood love for God. Unfortunately, she automatically transferred her perfectionist standards to her Christian life. Even after several years of enjoying Christian fellowship, she was still unable to shake her depression, because her self-esteem rested on the fragile balance of perfection. In addition to feeling like she had failed herself, she also felt that she had failed God. What a tremendous pressure to bear all those years! Once she untangled her own expectations from the Lord's call for her, her depression and discouragement diminished significantly. Her perfectionist ideals could no longer be tyrants that ruled her life. By adjusting her standards for measuring her worth, Miriam came to know God's love more fully, to accept his forgiveness and his strength.

Cathy also had unrealistically high ideals. A married woman with two young children, she was convinced that something was wrong with her life. It seemed to lack the joy she had seen in other women's lives. After we discussed her situation, it became evident that Cathy had rigidly defined what it meant to be a good Christian mother. Her definition was impossible for her, or for anyone, to live up to.

As a child, Cathy had always dreamed of being a wife and mother. She had often played that she was the "mother." And she lived most of her life anticipating the time when she would marry and raise her own children. Over the years an ideal of motherhood evolved that combined elements from her own fantasy, her mother's ideals, and impressions she picked up from television family shows. Once she began having children, she tried very hard to achieve her ideal. Her standard demanded that she be eternally patient, that she always love being with the children, and that she have fun with them every day. Of course, this model left no room for human nature, weakness, and the natural differences between adults and children.

As we talked about the problem, Cathy began to understand her ideals, where they came from and their potential to be helpful or detrimental to her life. Realistic ideals could motivate her to be a loving mother, raising her children in the ways of the Lord. But unrealistic ideals served only to frustrate her. Once she adjusted her standards, Cathy's original complaint of joylessness was remedied. Her sense of worth increased when she began to allow herself to be an adult human being, not a plastic, eternally smiling caricature of the perfect mother. She began to realize that the Lord didn't judge her by her old standards. Instead, he called her to rely on him for grace and strength to live the Christian life, rather than to rely on her own willpower. Her self-condemnation was replaced by a more realistic attitude towards herself and her children. As she felt better about herself, she grew to be a better and more joyful wife and mother.

The Christian Standard

If our ideals and expectations are out of order, they will hinder the Lord's work in our lives. It is common for women (and men, too) who maintain unrealistically high ideals to experience discouragement or to lead lives marked by a joyless striving to achieve impossible goals. Often, those goals and models become "Christianized." Of course, ideals do play an important part in our lives as Christians. Scripture repeatedly calls us to live a heroic life of love of God. For example, Paul encourages the Hebrews, saying, "Therefore, since we are surrounded by so great a cloud of witnesses, let us also lay aside every weight, and sin which clings so closely, and let us run with perseverance the race that is set before us, looking to Jesus the pioneer and perfecter of our faith, who for the joy that was set before him endured the cross, despising the shame, and is seated at the right hand of the throne of God" (Heb 12:1-2). Paul's exhortation is certainly an inspiration to love God with our whole heart. But many Christians respond to this call by acting like the Lord doesn't know we are imperfect. They either wallow in discouragement or resort to living by teeth-clenching willpower.

It takes a huge step to supplant our old standards with the new standard of Jesus Christ. Everything around us supports the world's idea that looks, brains, achievement, excellence, and personality are what's really important in life. Remember that the world's approval is elusive and leads only to momentary happiness and eventual frustration. There's always someone who can outshine us, someone more beautiful, more brilliant, and more gracious.

Our sense of worth should be based on the knowledge that the Lord created us. We are good. We should measure our qualities, attitudes, and actions by asking ourselves: "Am I being like Jesus now? Are these the qualities that Paul encouraged the early Christians to acquire?" Our sense of worth must be rooted in the standard that the Lord sets for us, not in anyone else's. Our self-esteem should come from the conviction that we are doing right in the eyes of the Lord.

Scripture offers concrete examples of the kind of behavior and character traits that please the Lord. In fact, it would take an entire book to cover all these qualities and characteristics. But here are a few of the characteristics of a woman who is pleasing to God: She obeys the commandments of the Lord.

She puts away anger, wrath, malice, slander, and foul talk from her mouth (Col 3:8). She puts on, as God's beloved, compassion, kindness, lowliness, meekness, and patience, forebearing and forgiving others (Col 3:12-13). She is "well-attested for her good deeds, as one who has brought up children, shown hospitality, washed the feet of saints, relieved the afflicted, and devoted herself to doing good in every way" (1 Tm 5:10). We need to measure Christian character according to the Lord's standard, a standard that is reflected in scripture and in the lives of faithful Christians who have gone to the Lord before us. To do this will take time and determination.

Our sense of personal value should come from the knowledge that we are living good, holy, Christian lives, ones that please God. Do we love God? Yes. That is cause for feeling good about ourselves. Do we try to be kind and loving to those he has given us? Yes, we try. That also is cause for confidence. Do we repent of sin, and do we desire to live a righteous life? Yes, we do. The only mirror worth gazing into is the one that reflects Christ in us.

Low Standards Mean Low Motivation

Not everyone is motivated by idealistic standards. Some of us have the opposite problem. As children, we may have lacked the models we needed to help us form standards for our life. As a result we lack the motivation to become modeled after our Lord Jesus Christ.

Common to all Christians is the call to put off the old man (or woman) and put on the new. We are to put off sin and put on holiness. Without the personal conviction that we *can* grow in holiness, that we *can* be transformed into the image and likeness of Christ, it is very difficult to change. Lack of personal growth is often a sign that our standards or expectations for ourselves are too low.

Judy, for example, could never quite convince herself that it was worth the trouble to do whatever was necessary to change her life. The call to discipleship seemed a mountain too steep to scale, so she sat at the base of it discouraged. It frustrated her that women who had been Christians the same amount of time that she had seemed to have made greater progress in the Christian life. "What's wrong with me anyway?" she asked. Her discouragement was a symptom of the low ideals she held for her life.

Judy didn't have confidence in herself. She needed someone to believe in her, to have confidence that she *could* change. Their confidence could make up for her lack of confidence. But to whom could she look to for this kind of encouragement? First of all, she could look to the Lord himself. And she did.

Like Judy, we need to be utterly convinced that God believes we can live up to his standards. We know that he does because of what scripture says about his nature and the power of the Holy Spirit. Paul states plainly in Philippians, chapter 4, that we can do all things in him who strengthens us. We can do *all* things because the Lord is our strength, our rock, our stronghold. The Lord is not capricious. He doesn't say, "I call all of you to be holy like my Son but only give some of you the strength to be holy." He calls all of us and provides the strength and grace for all of us.

We also need another person to believe in us. I was that person for Judy. For you it may be another woman, who has offered to be your friend, or it may be your roommate or your husband. We all need someone to cheer us on, someone to say, "You can do it. Don't give up. It's worth the hassle. Trust in the Lord and rely on him."

Slowly but surely our low expectations will be replaced by realistic ones that reflect the Lord's standards for our lives. Fight discouragement. Remember, you can do all things in him who strengthens you!

Super-Christian

Ironically, to our human nature even the Christian ideal can be a stumbling block. An idealized picture of the "good Christian woman" often acts as an obstacle to the freedom we are to experience in Christ. It presents an image of perfection which leaves no room for sins, failures, mistakes, and short-comings. Who can measure up to such an ideal? No human being that I know. So where does that leave us? Should we give up? It seems that we are doomed to fail when we measure ourselves according to the world's standard. We can be thankful that God has provided a way out of this dilemma. He has given us his own Son, who through his death and resurrection made reparation for our sins. Jesus has overcome *every* barrier that separates us from the Father. He has made peace between sinful, finite human beings and their perfect infinite Creator. He has given us an ideal to be a beacon of light guiding us through life, inspiring us to overcome sin and weakness, to live a life worthy of his calling. But, because he knows our weakness better than anyone, he has made provision for us when we fall short of the ideal. When we are weak, we can seek him for the grace and the strength to overcome our weakness. We can ask forgiveness when we sin.

Emotions and Super-Christian

How does the perfectionist model affect our emotions? It's easy to see that it can tyrannize our lives. Our "ideal Christian woman" always has a cheery "praise the Lord" for everything that happens to her or anyone else. Those rare occasions when she does share about having a difficult time always happen *after* she's overcome her difficulty and learned *so* many wonderful things through it. She never has any uncomfortable emotions like anger, jealousy, or fear. She never feels rebellious or frightened. And she certainly never cries herself to sleep. This ideal of perfection can become a one-dimensional model, an albatross around our necks, as we face the limitations in our daily lives. When we look at our fears, hopes, and dreams next to her super-Christian performance, we seem to be second-rate spiritual citizens.

Women often hold on to a super-Christian ideal. When they encounter in themselves unacceptable emotions such as envy, selfishness, or depression they quickly deal those emotions a death blow. The hurried burial of distasteful emotions is called repression. But God gave us our emotions, and repression is simply an ineffective way of handling them. It takes a lot of energy to keep these feelings buried and to continue striving for an unrealistic level of emotional "freedom."

Another common way for us to handle Super-Christian's presence in our lives is to respond by becoming discouraged and depressed when we face our own shortcomings and negative feelings. When our sin and weakness become painfully obvious to us, our judgment is swift—we have not only failed ourselves but God. We need to reject these unrealistic spiritual models just as we reject worldly models. This happy, always even-tempered model is a fiction; there is certainly no basis in scripture for it.

Let's stop bowing down to the idol of perfectionism. God already knows what we feel and think; it's impossible to keep a secret from him. If our ideal of the "model Christian" contradicts the real, eternal foundation the Lord wants to build in us, we've got to get rid of it.

When parents watch their sons and daughters take their first steps, they rejoice over their children's effort and appreciate the few faltering steps they do manage. The Lord looks at our attempts to resist sin and to overcome failures and shortcomings in much the same way. He sees that love motivates our effort, and he approves our desire to keep living the Christian life, despite our failure. He forgives our sin, encourages our efforts, and praises our successes.

We err if we confuse the standards set by ourselves or others with those the Lord asks us to live by. When we meet the sin within us, we should not respond with discouragement or with iron-strong willpower. Instead we should ask for and receive God's forgiveness. Whenever we see weakness in our lives, we should ask the Lord for strength and grace to overcome it.

Stepping Out of the Trap of Low Self-Esteem

Regardless of whether you grapple with low self-esteem regularly or only occasionally, several things can help you deal with it. Let me list them briefly.

1. Consider the standards by which you measure yourself. Write them down. Now ask yourself what standards and expectations the Lord has for you. Write those down. Do the lists match? If not, decide today that you will no longer evaluate your worth by the world's standards. Resolve to see yourself as a daughter of the Lord, loved by the Father.

2. Accept the fact that you're a human being. Admit that you are not perfect and never will be, but that God loves you. He forgives you and empowers you to live the Christian life.

3. Replace your inaccurate self-evaluation with a more accurate one. Ask one or two trusted Christian friends to write down or to tell you your strengths and virtues. (Do it even though you would rather not.) Then believe what they say.

4. Accept the fact that God loves *you*. You are his beloved. He finds you beautiful and is delighted that he created you. Read scripture to discover God's love and care for you. Picture yourself as someone that God loves when you come before him in prayer.

5. Accept compliments when they are given. Only false humility refuses encouragement and support when it is offered. When someone says you did something well, say thank you. Period. Don't try to discredit yourself or them by saying that it wasn't very good, really. If someone says you have pretty eyes, accept their opinion and admit that you have pretty eyes. God often uses brothers and sisters in the Lord as instruments of healing, and we need to receive that healing.

6. Discipline your thought life and the way you think about yourself. When old thought patterns of self-hatred and self-criticism crop up or when you begin to compare yourself or compete with others, stop and remember who you are in the eyes of the Lord. Remember who your brothers and sisters have said you are.

It Takes Patience

A good self-image isn't something you can acquire in a day, as you would acquire a new dress. Transforming a poor, inaccurate self-image into a stronger, confident, more accurate one can take years of faithfully speaking the truth to yourself. It takes time to substitute realistic, mature goals and ideals for the pie-in-the-sky ones that lead only to self-condemnation and frustration.

While we are growing in self-esteem, we can expect the evil one to oppose us in every possible way. Remember, he is known as the accuser of the brethren (Rv 12:10). He loves to rub salt into already sore wounds, and he is only too willing to agree with our low estimation of ourselves. He will only too quickly try to rob us of victory as we build our self-esteem. He will tell us that to think well of ourselves is to be prideful. So be aware that this area, as any other, is a battleground, and we are the prize. As the Lord calls us into freedom, the evil one will do his best to ensnare us in self-hatred.

As our relationship with the Lord grows stronger, and as we bring our thoughts into harmony with the mind of God, we will become more confident. We will be women who know that God loves them and who are therefore worthy. We will be able to live the Christian life more effectively. We will be able to love and serve God and others with more freedom and power. Problems with inferiority, isolation, anxiety, depression, and self-hatred will become less of a handicap as we grow in love and service to God.

Father, I need to know that I am your daughter. Reveal to me the beauty of your creation in me. I know that I am nothing by myself but with you, O Lord, I can live in security and fulfillment.

FIVE

We Have Bodies Too

MANY OF US think of ourselves as spiritual beings who are only incidentally housed in a physical shell. Consequently, we might try to live our Christian lives as if we were only spirit, forgetting that we have bodies too. But this approach creates problems. It produces men and women who do their best to pretend that their physical natures do not affect their lives as Christians.

If we fail to consider the fact that we are physical beings as well as spiritual beings, we won't be able to deal with our emotions effectively. We must realize that our physical selves have a very powerful and direct influence on our emotions and, therefore, on our lives as Christians.

The Lord doesn't ignore the fact that we are physical creatures as well as spiritual ones. After all, he was the one who made us that way. Then why do some Christians act as if the body is evil? The problem stems from confusion over the way that scripture commonly uses the word *flesh*. The common usage of *flesh* indicates the rebellious, sinful parts of our nature, "the old man." Yet many people think that it directly refers to our physical nature. But scripture affirms that the physical shell, our body, is good and created by God himself. The flesh that scripture usually refers to consists of desires and actions that are unredeemed and contrary to the will of God.

In an effort to "overcome the flesh," some of us mistakenly try to ignore our physical selves. We attempt to relate to the Lord as if we were pure spirit. Continuing to serve others while excessively fatigued, skipping too many meals as a form of fasting, failing to schedule recreation and relaxation time in our week because it seems selfish—all these are ways of ignoring our bodies. Such actions will not make us more holy, but will only serve to undermine our health and make us irritable and cross. Our health can either give us energy to do the things that we need to do, or it can hamper our ability to serve God and others. Whether we like it or not, our physical selves are here to stay. The best way to relate to that fact is to understand how they affect us. Then we can use that understanding to live a holy and righteous life.

Body Consciousness

There are three main approaches to body consciousness. A common one is to ignore our bodies. We either don't like what we see or find it confusing. So we decide not to think about it. Bodies seem to get in the way of life. Wouldn't everything be much simpler if we could cut off our "selves" from the neck down? We ignore physical symptoms or attend to them hurriedly in order to get on with life, especially when they have to do with a specifically feminine problem.

On the other end of the spectrum are those of us who are overly body-conscious. We may have a heightened awareness or concern for ourselves—either for our looks or our physical well-being. Often, this concern becomes paramount, so that our relationship with the Lord no longer takes first place. The world's standard of how we should feel and look encourages and stimulates our self-concern. As a result, we focus a disproportionate amount of attention on ourselves.

But, as Christian women, we needn't be locked into either of these extremes. We can embrace a more balanced and practical approach—the Lord's approach. Remember, God created us as physical beings. It is through our bodies that we enjoy God's creation: food, rest, and the beauties of nature, as well as human warmth and affection. Of course we can become so concerned with our bodies that they become idols to us. Or we can try to ignore our bodies, but that is to deny the fact that God gave them to us for a purpose. Our bodies are meant to serve us just as our emotions are. We should care for them in a way that allows us to serve God effectively.

Beauty

The way a woman rates her physical beauty in relation to other women can often be a source of anxiety, depression, and self-hatred. The advertising world's standard of beauty and desirability can make a woman dissatisfied with herself and encourage her to compete with other women. This competition can ruin relationships among Christian women by turning each woman in on herself. Dissatisfaction and discontent at not meeting the world's standards of physical beauty are often at the root of some of the emotional difficulties we experience.

Does this mean that we should take no concern for how we look? On the contrary, the balanced approach takes concern for appearance and hygiene, while being vigilant that such concern does not become obsessive or competitive. Moreover, it should not be based on the world's ideal. We should develop an alternate standard of attractiveness, one based on inner qualities. The time and effort we spend on our appearance should be balanced by our concern to become beautiful to the Lord. Our goal is not to be sexy, to be drawing attention to ourselves, but to become pleasing in the eyes of God. At the same time, we should not disdain physical beauty. As we focus on developing a heart of love and service, our physical beauty will inevitably grow. Once we develop the proper priorities, the time we spend on our appearance will fall into the right balance.

Hormones and Our Emotions

A book directed to women has the advantage of allowing us to spend time, woman to woman, discussing the way we experience life in a cyclical pattern. Although our menstrual period comes approximately once a month, the rest of the days in the month are also very directly influenced by our hormonal cycle.

Men have one hormone, testosterone, that provides the chemical basis for their sexual behavior. Women, on the other hand, have both estrogen and progesterone interrelating throughout their lives. The menstrual cycle is a complex sequence of hormonal activity.

During the first stage of the menstrual cycle, the estrogen level increases gradually until it reaches a level that signals the release of the ovum or egg. After the egg has been released, progesterone is produced and increases until it reaches a level that signals the onset of the menstrual flow.

Many studies indicate that the cyclical rhythm of a woman's hormones directly influences her self-image and her emotions. When we were growing up, we may have heard mumblings about premenstrual tension, which we may have considered simply an old wives' tale. But scientific research shows evidence that a direct correlation exists between hormone function and a woman's emotions. Depression, irritability, anxiety, and hostility have been noted as significant symptoms of premenstrual high progesterone levels. These feelings decline and often disappear completely at the onset of menstruation. During ovulation and midway in the cycle, a woman usually experiences well-being and confidence and a notable lack of anxiety and hostility. Recently, the medical profession has concluded that water retention and calcium depletion are just two of many physical factors that contribute to mood swing during the last one-third of the cycle.

Why This Concern?

I've taken the opportunity to explain the correlation between hormones and emotions because women often discount or discredit the fact that they experience life differently at one time of the month than another. They assume that there is little objective reason why they should experience their emotions any differently than men do. But, if they persist in ignoring the fact that the cyclical nature of their hormonal life affects them, they will experience life as an unpredictable series of highs and lows, which they are left to fight by their own willpower.

It is not a character flaw or weakness to have a nature that is cyclical rather than linear. We should not fight the facts but cooperate with them. Here are some guidelines to help us work with our nature rather than against it.

1. Begin to keep track of your cycle accurately. I find it helpful to mark this on my planning calendar so I don't have to keep track of another piece of paper. When did you start menstruating this month? How many days since your last menses?

2. Record any significant mood swings or physical symptoms, and note when they occurred. "All this week I was full of energy"; "Boy, have I been a crab for the last few days"; "headache"; "diarrhea."

3. Try to see if a pattern emerges over a period of months.

How does it help to know what's going on in our cycle? It helps because such knowledge offers another opportunity to take the mystery out of our emotions. If they always seem to have a mind of their own and always catch us on our blind side, we will continue to be prey to them rather than to be their master. The more we know about the things that affect our emotions, the stronger and freer we will be to love and serve God, to enjoy the life he has given us.

It helps to know that our premenstrual syndrome is hormonally stimulated. A woman can get very discouraged with her progress in controlling her temper if she loses her "cool" and becomes angry every three or four weeks. Her behavior, the result of premenstrual strain, can make her angry, self-condemning, or depressed when she is faced with her apparent backsliding. Understanding how her hormones affect her emotions can prevent a woman from being too harsh on herself.

This self-knowledge doesn't necessarily excuse us. We still have to take responsibility for our emotions. If we make an unkind remark to someone, we should admit our sin but temper it with the knowledge that we have a lower resistance to sin in this area just a few days before menstruation. Self-knowledge can also prevent us from falling into wrongdoing. Perhaps we notice on our calendar that our period is due in a week. We can make a mental resolve to guard against the temptation to sin through anger. We can redouble our efforts to be patient and understanding, even though it will be harder than usual for us to do so.

We should also turn confidently to the Lord, expecting him to give us strength and grace to be his loving servants. If we tend to feel depressed and insecure the week before menstruation, we should ask the Lord to help us keep our thoughts off ourselves so that we can keep a proper, accurate perspective on life.

Along with resolving to resist temptation and asking the Lord for strength, we can exercise mental discipline. Rather than letting depressing thoughts run through our mind, we should summon all our strength to guard our mind, the gateway to our emotions. We should remember to have substitute thoughts and scriptures ready to help us redirect our thoughts. Even if we've struggled for years with premenstrual symptoms, we can confidently expect to experience greater stability as we take control of ourselves and appropriate the power of the Holy Spirit in this area of our lives.

Perspective is one of my favorite words, especially for women. Because of our cyclical nature, it's particularly important that we look not only at part of our life but at the whole of it. It's easy to become convinced that we are emotional basket cases if we judge ourselves according to the last few days preceeding our period, rather than on our behavior the rest of the month.

Francine, a woman in her early thirties, was a mature, confident, capable wife and mother, most of the time. She knew herself fairly well and had gathered that she was a better than average wife and mother, who coped well with the demands on her life. But once in a while she would end up in tears, bemoaning her utter failure to love her children the way she should. Her husband, confused by her tears but trying to understand what was going on with his wife, reminded her of recent occasions on which she had handled the children exceptionally well. But she could list ten failures for every one of his encouragements, and this only drove her to more tears. As she cried herself to sleep, she wondered how her husband, who was so good, could love her anyway.

A few days later her husband, who was still concerned for her, asked how she was doing. Looking a bit surprised, she said that she was just fine. After several episodes, she and her husband began to see a link between the time of her period and her lapse into depression and negative thinking. After that, her husband could encourage her when she became a bit teary eyed by reminding her that it was the week before her period. With that knowledge, she didn't have to give full credibility to her feelings, and she was able to get through those difficult few days until she could see things more clearly herself.

Self-Evaluation

Women commonly try to evaluate themselves and their worth during the time preceeding their period. But this is probably the worst time for self-evaluation or for making major life changes. If a decision or change needs to be made, postpone it if possible until after the days immediately preceding your period are over. Once your progesterone level lowers, your perspective will be more accurate and life will seem more reasonable. Anxiety and depression will also be at their lowest ebb at that time.

It can help to plan your activities during the month in a way that takes account of how you are likely to feel physically. Take advantage of the mid-month surge of energy by planning to shampoo the carpets or re-pot all the plants or do heavy cleaning at that time. Since energy levels, both physical and emotional, are down during the premenstrual days, take it a bit easy on yourself if you can. Don't overextend yourself by trying to accomplish too much. It will only feed any predisposition to irritability and self-condemnation you may have. Extra rest at this time can help you to cope with small children or with situations that require more self-control and patience.

Again, balance is the key when it comes to gaining more

knowledge about ourselves as women. No one is helped when
we become intrigued with ourselves and self-concerned. Any
signs of self-concern should caution us to stop thinking about
ourselves lest we fall into the trap of self-pity and introspection.
It's good to know ourselves, but it's not good to become
introspective.

Just because we may sometimes need to take our menstrual
cycle into account doesn't mean that we treat ourselves as
invalids either. Responsibilities, jobs, and children are with us
every day. We should use our knowledge about ourselves
wisely, to enable us to be stronger and more effective all month
long.

Whether affected by our hormones or by circumstances, our
emotions need to be ruled by whatever is the "right" thing to do
at the moment. It's not a sin to feel on edge and irritable, but it is
a sin to act on those feelings. It's not wrong to feel depressed as
long as our actions do not lead to uncharitable behavior or to sin
against hope in God. The fact that hormones affect us doesn't
mean that they are more powerful than we are. As women whose
faith rests in God, we know that our unruly emotions can
become subject to his authority through prayer, discipline,
self-knowledge, and the support of others.

Pregnancy and childbirth also have a profound effect on the
level of hormones in our system. What I have said about the
connection between hormones and emotions holds true for
pregnancy and childbirth as well. Several good books are
available that can help you to understand the physical and
emotional changes that happen to a woman at these times. It can
help to ask other women about their experience. Self-
knowledge, the understanding that our emotions should be our
servants, and the willingness to rely on God and the support of
other Christian women are essential ingredients for learning
how to handle the effect that physical changes have on our lives.

Menopause

Menopause, or what is commonly referred to as the change of
life, is yet another time in a woman's life when hormonal

changes affect her physically and emotionally. Menopause results from the gradual decline of estrogen output that happens when a woman gets older. Besides the fact that menstruation gradually decreases and then stops entirely, a change occurs in the tissues of the genital organs and in the secondary sexual characteristics. In addition, there is a host of psychological and bodily related symptoms that can accompany menopause: headaches, dizziness, hot flashes, depression, confusion and inability to concentrate, crying spells, and irritability.

Let's admit that for most of us, the thought of menopause brings fear and anxiety. Some women make menopause sound like an experience akin to medieval torture. Such fears are contagious and can prevent us from approaching menopause with expectant faith and hope.

Another reason for our fear stems from the world's standard for beauty and self-worth: being young and beautiful is equated with what's best in life. Menopause indicates that we are growing older and entering another stage of our lives. If we are insecure about growing old and becoming less attractive according to the world's standard, we may frantically try to deny the changes that are going on in us. Here is another area for which we, as Christians, need to develop an alternate standard of respect and honor, self-esteem and contentment. Everyone's a loser according to the world's standard. But with the Lord, every stage of our lives brings something new and beautiful.

Menstruation signals that our bodies are ready for the time of life that requires building and creating a home and a family. As young married women, our bodies are geared to bear and raise children. It is good to honor and rejoice in that special time of life when we are in it. Menopause signals an end to one stage or season of our lives and heralds another one. Usually by the time a woman begins menopause, some of her children are raised and have begun to leave home. The fact that the physical and emotional effects of menopause coincide with the children leaving home compounds what is sometimes called the menopausal crisis. It's not coincidence that these two events occur at roughly the same time. One time in a woman's life is ending—but life is not ending. A new time of life is beginning.

Here are suggestions given by older sisters in the Lord. It's important to incorporate these principles into our thinking.

1. Menopause is a natural change and not some "big thing" that is happening to you.

2. The Lord can become more of a source of strength and life as you draw close to him.

3. Caring for your health is very important. Exercise—walking, swimming, tennis—helps to control many of the symptoms such as fatigue, depression, wakefulness, and severe emotional swings.

4. Fellowship with other Christian women who are going through the same things (be sure it's not a complaining session) can help keep life in proper perspective.

Fatigue and Illness

Fatigue and illness are other physical conditions that affect our emotions. Fatigue can often lead to depression and loss of control over our emotions. It is common for a woman who lacks sleep or rest to become irritable and jumpy or depressed and melancholy. Everything looks a bit worse and seems a bit more overwhelming. It takes an immense amount of energy to deal with and control certain emotions that could have been better handled by taking a nap or getting to bed early. It's easy to overlook our human condition and to assume that the cause of a disordered emotional life is always a spiritual one.

Illness can have a similar effect on us. A cold or the flu can upset our normally well-ordered lives. Instead of being harsh with ourselves, we may need to be a bit more understanding and loving towards ourselves. Our resistance may be down, and we may be prone to irritability or depression. On the other hand, if we treat ourselves too gingerly, we will fall into the trap of self-concern. It's important to have a balanced diet, to get rest and exercise, to get proper medical attention when necessary. And of course we should always turn to the Lord for healing, strength, and perseverance.

Fatigue and illness can sometimes be signs that our bodies are trying to tell us something. We may need to slow down, to reorder our priorities. Perhaps we need to take better care of ourselves or get medical help or deal with a problem with anxiety. Our bodies are God's gifts; they are supposed to help us live the good life he intended us to have.

Therefore, as women of God, let us present ourselves as temples of the Holy Spirit, living sacrifices to God. We should care for the bodies he gave us. We should resolve not to bow before our bodies as idols or to treat them with disrespect. As with every aspect of our lives, we should bring our bodies before the Lord, seeking his wisdom and discernment about how we can better serve him and his people.

Lord in heaven, give me understanding and direction so that my physical nature will serve your plan for my life. My life is yours, Father. My only desire is to do your will here on earth, for I love you.

SIX

Emotions— Master or Servant?

BEFORE WE DISCUSS specific emotions, it will help to outline a general approach to our emotions. This outline will provide the perspective on which later chapters will build.

As Christians, we know that God made us—yes, our emotions too. And he saw that what he had made was good. As with everything God created, our emotions are to have a positive and fruitful function in our lives.

What exactly are emotions? Emotions are reactions within us to situations, people, and things. The word "emotion" comes from the Latin *movere*, which means to move or to move from one place to another. Our emotions are meant to move us to action. They are also meant to function as signals that alert us to something. Fear of being in an automobile accident, for example, can motivate us to fasten our seat belts and lock the car door. In this situation, fear functions as God intended; it works *for* us by protecting us from injury.

At other times, our emotions simply indicate things to us. Like road signs on a highway, they tell us that we need to pay attention to a series of rough spots or curves in our lives. For instance, depression can be a sign that something is not working right. We can't afford to ignore this sign if we want to overcome the depression. Grief can tell us that someone or something that we care about is no longer present in our lives. Loneliness may be a sign that we need to do something about pursuing friendships, or it may indicate that we are indulging in self-pity. We need to pay attention to these signals along the way. They are like the warning lights on the dashboard of a car.

Unfortunately, because of our fallen nature, our emotions can also motivate or move us in negative and less helpful ways. We must realize that, as a result of the Fall, our emotions are no longer working as God originally intended. They have been affected by sin and death, which entered the world when man disobeyed God. Consequently, they cannot be relied upon to prompt us to do what is right in every situation. To illustrate this point, let us look at fear again. In the above example, fear motivated us to protect ourselves from being injured. But suppose that we begin to fear other people. Such fear can cause us to withdraw and become anxious, to isolate and separate us from the people God has given us to love and care for. Or, again, the feeling of attraction to another person, which should motivate us as God intended to get married and raise children, could also motivate us to become involved in an adulterous relationship.

In themselves, our emotions are neither good nor bad. But they can have good or bad effects, depending on how we handle them. In order to have a healthy emotional life, we need to begin by accepting our emotions as God's gift to us.

Of course, many other related factors contribute to the conflict between the way we handle our emotions and our basic intent to do good. Many of us lacked proper training as children, or experienced some traumatic events that have affected our emotional makeup. We may lack self-control, or we may never have been exposed to clear Christian teaching regarding our emotions. For these and other reasons, we grow to adulthood not knowing how to handle them. But, regardless of our past experience, we can learn to handle our emotions according to God's plan.

As children of God we are much more than just a physical shell designed to house a wide array of emotions. We are more than our feelings. But we are commonly told, often by practioners of popular psychology, that *we are our emotions*. A number of writers say that our emotions are the most important part of our lives, and some authors present some very persuasive arguments to support their case. Such an approach encourages us to pay undivided attention to our feelings and to give our emotions unlimited credibility. We have all heard statements like the following:

> Being in touch with your feelings is the only way you can ever become your highest self, the only way you can become open and free, the only way you can become your own person. . . . If you don't live in your feelings, you don't live in the real world. Feelings are the truth. (David Viscott, *The Language of Feelings* [New York: Pocket Books, 1977], p. 137)

Guided by this kind of thinking, our *selves* soon become the most important thing in the world. We begin to believe that our feelings should determine our actions and that there is no such thing as objective moral truth to guide our lives. This erosion of Christian principles is especially pronounced in the area of sexual freedom. Take this statement, for example.

> But something is holding you back from expressing those [sexual] wants freely. That something is often known as morality. Which isn't surprising, since most of us expect morality to limit our lives. But this doesn't have to be so. Your morality can lift you, liberate you, in many ways. How? By affirming freedom instead of conventionality. No matter what people say, no act is immoral if it has no victim. And no act good unless it brings pleasure. (George Weinberg, *Self-Creation* [New York: St. Martin's Press, 1978], p. 137)

As Christians, we know that such a statement contradicts basic Christian truth. The only one who can truly liberate us is Jesus Christ. All acts are good if they please God, regardless of whether they please us. Although an important part of us, our emotions are not everything. We need to put them in proper perspective so that they do not have a greater place in our lives than God intended.

Fact, Faith, and Feelings

Campus Crusade for Christ often uses a train diagram to explain the place of fact, faith, and feelings in the Christian life. The engine of the train is *fact*, the middle car is *faith*, and the caboose is *feelings*. If we put our faith in the fact—in the truth—our feelings will follow in proper order. The truth, and not our feelings, provides the motive power for our lives; it is the engine that pulls the train.

Fact—What is the truth of the gospel?
Faith—Faith teaches that we have the power to respond in accordance with the truth.
Feelings—Our emotions are intended to serve the truth. Once truth and faith are operating properly, our emotions will get in line where they belong.

Let's try a concrete example. Suppose you're feeling that no one loves you. You know that you're far from being the "model" Christian woman. In fact, you're acutely aware of your own shortcomings. You begin to feel that God couldn't possibly love you. You could simply wallow in your sense of dejection, becoming alienated from those around you, or you could follow the fact, faith, feeling approach.

Fact—God loves you. His own Son suffered and died so you could be reconciled to him. If you've done something wrong, you can repent and receive the forgiveness that God so generously offers.

Faith—Even though the circumstances seem to point in the opposite direction, you believe that God's love for you is steady; it never changes. His picture of you is the *real* one.

Feelings—Gradually, your feelings of isolation and rejection give way to ones of gratefulness and love for God because of what he's done for you.

In the first instance, if you made your feelings the engine, your life would begin to career out of control, until you found yourself depressed and lonely. In the second, you've based your life on the truth and found that it sets you free from the tyranny of your emotions.

Let's consider a second example. You become furious when one of your children disobeys. You need to know the right way to act. If you let your anger take over, it may lash out in destructive ways which you will later regret. But if you take the faith, fact, feelings approach you will relate to the guilty child with the sense of true justice that the Lord will give you. And you will find that sometimes the problem is with you, not the child.

Our faith in Christ and his promises gives us the confidence that, no matter how weak we are, no matter how overwhelming our feelings seem, we have the power, in the name of Jesus and through the gift of his Holy Spirit, to act according to the truth. As Paul says, "I can do all things in him who strengthens me" (Phil 4:13).

Our feelings come last in the train diagram because they cannot always be trusted to lead us in the right direction. When we are happy and full of energy, it's easy to feel like loving and serving others. But what about the days when we don't "feel" so loving? Christ never said to love others only when you feel like it. He said, "Love others as I have loved you!"

That is why our actions should be ruled by the truth of the gospel and empowered by the Holy Spirit. When our feelings coincide with the facts and with our faith, hallelujah! But when they don't, we need to put them in a subordinate or secondary position in our lives.

Friend or Enemy?

God intends our emotions to serve us. We are to master them rather than let them control us. Unfortunately, most of us do not experience our emotions as our servants. Sometimes they seem more like petty tyrants, who subject us to their every whim. We feel helpless in the face of what appears to be such a strong and persistent force. One moment we are "up" and the next we are "down," tossed about like a toy boat on a stormy lake.

Fear of our emotions and their power over us often makes us mistrust ourselves. One woman I know said she experienced her emotions as a Dr. Jeckle and Mr. Hyde phenomenon. One day she was a reasonable, loving woman and the next day an irritable, nagging shrew. Such unpredictable behavior affects not only the person who displays it but everyone she comes into contact with.

But knowledge of God and his ways should give us mastery over every aspect of our lives. When our emotions conflict with the truth, we will need to discount them. If they urge us to tell someone off as a result of a real or imagined insult, we need to recognize that we are having an emotional reaction. We should first of all remember what the loving, Christlike thing to do is. Then we must subordinate our feelings and go ahead and do what's right.

Introspection: The Enemy of Emotional Health

Preoccupation with our feelings and emotions and a general fascination with ourselves is one of the common disorders of the twentieth century. This inwardness is a sure dead end for our spiritual lives. Introspection, the ongoing analysis of oneself, is a never-completed task. This self-dialogue can soon become the pervasive activity in life. We run the risk of dislodging Jesus from his position at the center of our lives and enthroning our emotions as the pivotal point of our existence. How *we* are, how *we* feel about something becomes the most important question. For a Christian, habitual introspection is simply not an acceptable lifestyle.

Obviously, this kind of self-fascination simply does not line up with what the gospel proclaims. Scripture is filled with the call to imitate Jesus. He is the only way approved by the Father.

According to scripture, a Christian's life should be filled with the love of God. Out of that love comes our second call, to love and serve each other (Mt 22:37-40). Clearly, scripture does not teach us to love and serve ourselves first and then others.

Besides the fact that self-preoccupation is incompatible with true Christian discipleship, the fact that introspection bears bad fruit is another sign that it is not healthy. At first it may lead down very attractive paths. The pleasure of being introspective can reinforce our desire to wander yet farther down the pathway of our feelings and our minds. Sometimes the result can be helpful, but often it is not. An abyss of memories, reactions, and feelings all coexist within our minds, some pleasant and others not. The unpleasant ones stir up more unpleasant ones, often bringing to the surface hurts, resentments, and memories that would be better off left alone, at least for the time being. The tendency to linger within ourselves, to emphasize whatever goes on within us, soon becomes disproportionate to the rest of life. Instead of solving the original problem, it usually uncovers and creates more. Melancholy and distraction are just some of the fruits of introspection.

Self-Knowledge Is Essential

Does this mean that a Christian woman should never examine her emotions? Should she keep a tight grip on everything that happens within her? Repression is no answer for a Christian. Then, what is? One of the most helpful tools for maintaining a healthy emotional balance for our Christian lives is what I call self-knowledge. Unlike introspection, the aim of self-knowledge is to acquire information about who we are and what we feel *specifically for the purpose of strengthening an area of our lives.* Like any good tool, self-knowledge is under our control. It does not operate on its own, delving into whatever areas it will, but it is at work where and when *we* will.

Let me offer an example to illustrate this point. Abby had problems with discontentment and anger. When she wanted something, she could make life miserable for everyone if she didn't get her way. Right now, she wasn't very happy about the kind of vacation she was going to have. How did she handle her disappointment? The usual way. She turned within herself and mused about her feelings. "I can't help being angry. My mother had the same problem with temper" (and a side-trip to remember mother's other bad habits). "And besides, I deserve a better vacation than last year's since I worked so hard at this crummy job." Such thoughts inevitably led to self-pity.

If Abby had turned from introspection and decided to approach her feelings about the vacation using self-knowledge, she might have wound up at a different place. "I'm feeling crummy about this vacation, and I'm taking it out on everyone. I want to stop acting like this, but I don't know if I can. My mother had this problem (avoid getting into "feelings about mother" here), and I've always handled situations that way too. I'm angry because what I want so badly might not happen. Next time I need to ask the Lord to show me when I begin to get angry. I really do believe that with the power of God I am not locked into this way of reacting."

Abby could then consider a more mature and Christlike way to handle threatening situations. Through self-knowledge, she could begin to understand why she felt the way she did, and she could take positive action to change her behavior. On her inward journey she would not have simply overturned every stone in her way, such as her feelings about her mother, but would have selectively and prudently chosen where her thoughts would take her. Some helpful tools can emerge from self-examination, particularly if we don't give every thought and feeling credibility but rather weigh them in the light of the Holy Spirit. We should not have an insatiable curiosity about our emotions, nor should we relate to them as powers and forces that are beyond our control, powers that we must do our best to ignore.

Jesus is the Master of our lives. Our emotions must be kept in their rightful place as our servants and Christ's servants. If we let them usurp the central position in our lives, they will be of little use to us, and, consequently, we will be of little service to

God. Our part is to let our emotions serve us by giving us the information we need to live the free and loving life that the Lord wants for us. If we do that, our lives will display the peace and power of Christ.

Lord, I thank you for the gift of my emotions. May they serve you and your kingdom. Teach me how to control them so that they might support, and not hinder, my life in you.

SEVEN

Be Angry but Sin Not

SCORES OF BOOKS and articles have been published over the last ten years and overwhelming the public with advice on handling anger. We've been advised to punch pillows and walls, to write hate letters and then tear them up, to pretend to telephone our enemies and yell nasty words at them while the line is dead. The general flow of counsel is to "let it all hang out."

Can a Christian accept this advice? Should we let our feelings rule us when it comes to dealing with anger? One reason why Christians so readily accept secular advice is that they lack clear Christian teaching about how to live their daily lives. There simply isn't much of it around. Because of the lack of clear contemporary teaching, some Christians swing to the other extreme and conclude that all anger is sinful and, therefore, something to studiously avoid.

Let's look at what scripture has to say about anger. The Bible refers frequently to anger, usually in one of two ways. It offers pastoral advice on expressing righteous anger, and it describes anger as a work of the flesh, as a sin.

Is Anger Always Wrong?

Anger is an emotion, and, like any emotion, it comes and goes. Of itself, anger is neither good nor bad. Our *response* to our angry feelings is what determines whether anger is a sin in any given situation. Aware of anger's potency, its power to destroy, hurt, or even kill, scripture gives us sober and specific advice for handling it.

In his letter to the Ephesians, Paul cautions the church to "Be angry but sin not," or, in another translation, "If you are angry, let it be without sin" (Eph 4:26). Along with the admonitions in Proverbs 16:32 and James 1:19 to control our anger, this passage seems to indicate that anger can be an acceptable emotion for the Christian. But it must be governed and controlled if it is not to lead us into sin.

Jesus himself expressed righteous anger. His anger was directed against wrongdoing. In Matthew, chapter 23, he calls the scribes and Pharisees "frauds," "vipers' nests," and a "brood of serpents." Surely these verses show that Jesus was angry and that he didn't hesitate to express his anger. "Vipers' nests" is hardly a conciliatory phrase!

In Mark's Gospel, Jesus becomes angry when those he is teaching in the synagogue close their minds to him and to the truth that he reveals (see 3:5). And in Matthew, one can hardly imagine Jesus overturning the tables and stalls of dove sellers in the temple calmly. He was angry!

Just as anger motivated Jesus to throw the money-changers out of the temple, our anger can motivate us to take action. These scripture passages support the conclusion that anger is not *in itself* sinful. This can be a tremendous relief for many Christians. Jesus' example points out that anger can be an appropriate response to sin and wrongdoing. Anger was not his only response to wrongdoing, but at times it was obviously the correct one.

As Christians, we ought to become angry when faced with some forms of sin, whether it is injustice done to others or to ourselves or disrespect towards God himself. Sometimes the correct response to sin is to go to our knees, quietly interceding for the difficulty. But at times we need to become angry, just as the Lord did.

Unrighteous Anger: The Work of the Flesh

The other way that scripture refers to anger and some of its manifestations, such as quick temper (Col 3:8), outbursts of rage (Gal 5:20), and harsh words (Eph 4:31), may be more familiar to us. When we speak about anger, most of us are probably referring to the way we feel when we lose patience or when people or things irritate us. This type of destructive anger expresses itself in two main ways: as "hot" anger (screaming, throwing things, fighting, and so on) or as "cold" anger (making sarcastic remarks, withdrawing, planning revenge). Whether you experience anger as "hot" or "cold," you need to learn how to control it rather than let it control you. Unfortunately, our anger often hurts other people. If our anger is out of control or in control of us, we need to bring it under the light and rule of the Holy Spirit.

Angry Feelings

"But I never get angry," you might say. Think again! Aren't there times when you feel crabby and annoyed? That's the same thing as feeling angry. Words like *crabby* and *annoyed* can act as disguises for anger. They make it sound better. But disguising your anger never helps you control it. You will need to be able to identify your feelings accurately before you can control them and respond to them constructively.

For those of us who are not in touch with how we feel, it's especially important to *begin* learning how to identify angry feelings and their source when they develop. "I hate to admit it, but I was so angry I could have screamed the moment I heard her talking about me behind my back." "I began to hate him for treating my brother like that." Learning to trace our angry feelings to specific people, situations, and events is not just an exercise in introspection. If we are to gain self-control, we have to know what we are attempting to control, and we need to know when we are most vulnerable to anger.

After we recognize that we feel angry, we need to *accept* the fact that we have angry feelings. If we don't, we'll either repress them or feel guilty about them. Both alternatives only complicate our emotions. Repression never gets rid of anger; it only postpones it. We'll have to face up to it sooner or later, probably in an even more destructive form. Guilt doesn't eliminate our anger either. It only means that we will have to deal with self-hatred as well as the original anger. We may not like our anger, but owning up to it puts us in the position of being honest with ourselves and the Lord. Only if we are honest can we get on with the business of dealing with our angry feelings.

Christians often develop a set of misconceptions about what constitutes appropriate feminine behavior: constant smiling, always pleasing others, never showing outward displeasure. These misconceptions foster an inaccurate stereotype of Christian womanhood. The truth is that Christian women should be able to express righteous anger when they are confronted with sin or disrespect for God. I believe that God's people would be much stronger and more effective if we understood and expressed our anger more appropriately.

"But Sin Not"

The Lord only asks of us what we can do, though he does ask of us more than we can accomplish simply by exercising our own willpower. He gives us his Holy Spirit to empower us despite our weakness. Without the power of the Holy Spirit, the strength of our own determination will prove ineffective. If we are to obey God's command to "be angry but sin not," we will need to understand two important factors: self-control and positive action.

To Christians who have been formed by the modern approach to emotions, the thought of applying self-control seems quite preposterous. Don't we all "know" it's harmful not to express our feelings in whatever way feels good? We could do psychological damage to ourselves if we didn't. This is just not true. It is harmful to repress anger. But it is not psychologically harmful to control and direct it in positive ways. Paul tells us that "God did not give us a spirit of timidity but a spirit of power and love and self-control" (2 Tm 1:7). If God had not given us the ability to master our anger, he would not have commanded us to "get rid of all bitterness, all passion and anger, harsh words, slander, and malice of every kind" (Eph 4:31). Neither would Paul have said, "You should live in accord with the Spirit and you will not yield to the cravings of the flesh [to anger]" (Gal 5:16).

When anger surges up in us, attempting to express itself in unrighteous ways (by verbal and physical abuse or by withdrawal and sarcasm), we can say: "I don't have to do this; I can decide not to withdraw"; "I can choose not to yell at my husband." We can turn to the Lord, confident that his grace can overcome our weakness. But to do this, we need to have an alternate, *positive* way of expressing our anger.

Let's consider some of the most common sources of the anger that women experience. Then we can begin to express and handle our anger in a positive way. We shouldn't be afraid to identify the sources of our anger. This kind of self-knowledge can only bring us greater freedom. If we take a few moments to backtrack, we can discover the people or situations that trigger our angry feelings. Then we can identify situations that make us most vulnerable to sinning in this area.

Expectations

We should start by considering the expectations we have for ourselves and others. When we or others fail to live up to our expectations, we may respond in anger. "Can't you remember anything I ask you to do?" "If I make that same mistake one more time, I'll throw the whole thing out."

If we are to live in this imperfect world without developing ulcers, we are going to have to adjust our goals so that they become more realistic. If we do this, and if we exert self-control and make use of the power of the Holy Spirit, we will find that we no longer respond with anger every time we face our own or someone else's imperfections. Instead, we will develop the virtue of patience. We can pray for this fruit of the Spirit as we develop it in ourselves with self-discipline and realistic standards.

One mother of four shared her experience of anger with me:

Anger has been one area of my life that I've really had to work against. It expresses itself in little things, the small irritations of everyday life. For instance, when the kids would take dirty dishes out of the dishwasher and put them into the cabinet, I would just blow up. My husband helped me to overcome this anger by getting me to see through it. He would say, "What are you getting so upset about? Aren't you putting all this a little out of context?" I had to admit that I was making the whole thing bigger than it really was.

Once I finally admitted that, I began to realize that the root of my anger was selfishness. I wanted things *my* way. I wanted to have everything in exactly the right place, everything perfect and clean. To accomplish this, I made unnecessary demands on others. I had to realize that *I was expecting too much*, not only for myself, but for those I lived with. It was more than was humanly possible. When my expectations weren't fulfilled, I became angry.

I believe that if you want to learn how to handle your anger, you really have to find out why you are getting angry. A passage in Ephesians was an inspiration to me. "Never have grudges against others, or lose your temper, or raise your voice to anybody" (Eph 4:31). I wanted to be a very soft-spoken, gentle woman. But here I was yelling at the kids. This scripture passage would help me control my anger because it reminded me that I shouldn't respond by yelling, even when things upset me.

Communication Is Crucial

Communication is an important factor. Many of us were taught to avoid confrontation or conflict. We may never have learned to handle things one at a time, as they occur. In an effort to be "Christian" or to "keep peace" or to be a "nice person," we may swallow our anger. But this approach doesn't solve anything. Our anger will build until we either blow up over some small thing or until we develop an ulcer. We have never learned that good communication is a key to dealing with angry feelings.

Difficult situations don't simply go away, no matter how much we wish they would. Paul advises the Ephesians to "be angry but sin not. Do not let the sun go down on your anger and give the devil a foothold." Paul's advice, that we not let the sun go down on our anger, provides us with a tool for keeping our relationships free of sin.

My husband Randy and I have applied that verse literally in our marriage. And because of that scripture verse, our relationship does not bear the scars that many marriages do. By dealing with anger daily—as it comes up—resentment, hostility, and grudges have no opportunity to take root. "See to it that no one fail to obtain the grace of God; that no 'root of bitterness' spring up and cause trouble" (Heb 12:15).

This advice for dealing with anger can seem threatening and even overwhelming at first. Most of us don't even know how to start to "clean house" when it comes to our emotions. My advice is that we simply *start*. Only by swallowing our pride and overcoming our self-consciousness will we ever experience the freedom and peace that this spiritual principle provides. Only then will we gain the confidence we need to make this approach a way of life.

One friend of mine confesses:

I used to think that I was someone who didn't have any trouble with anger. Then I began to recognize that my anger was hidden. When I was angry I usually dealt with it by being quiet, keeping it all to myself. Of course, this meant that it would have to come out eventually. Sooner or later I would explode about something. Then it would take a while before I could repent and get things cleared up.

Now, whenever I become angry, I try to say something right away. When my husband and I first realized that anger was a difficulty for me, he asked me to say something even if I was angry over some simple thing or even if I expressed my anger in a negative way. I had to recognize the anger before I could get it out of my system.

Recently, I had a serious disagreement with my husband. I was surprised at myself, because I was able to look at him and say, "I am really mad!" "I am very angry." It didn't solve anything, but I was glad that I was able to express it. At the same time, I was tempted to say some pretty hard things to him. But something inside me said, "Don't say that; that's not true. You're going to regret it if you say it. Tell him you're angry, but don't say all that other stuff." I resisted the temptation to drag in things that had nothing to do with the situation at hand. What a victory that was for me! I had resisted making a whole series of exaggerated statements, which were generated by my feelings. Instead, I was able to express my anger in a way that I wouldn't regret later.

My husband and I weren't able to finish our conversation right then, so he called me later and we were able to work the whole thing out. I'm glad that I'm able to express my anger now. I'm no longer afraid of it, because I realize that it can sometimes be right to be angry. As long as it's expressed in a good way, I know that my anger can even bear good fruit.

Like my friend, most of us need to learn how to recognize and accept our angry feelings and to communicate about them constructively.

Holding on to Anger

Very few things fuel the fires of anger so much as harboring and nurturing the hurts and wrongs done to us in the past. Bitterness and resentment only contribute to deep feelings of anger.

Holding on to hurt and resentment is not the same thing as failing to communicate our anger because we don't know how to. In the latter case we are ignorant of the spiritual principle of Ephesians 4:26. We hold on to our anger because we don't know how to communicate it. But in the former, we deliberately *choose* to remain angry because we feel justified in doing so. It's easy to justify angry feelings towards people who have hurt us, towards "life" in general, and even towards God. We can dwell on the depth of the wrong or the need for revenge or the "unfairness" of the situation. In fact, there are so many opportunities to remember real or imagined wrongs that it would be easy to become a very angry person. If we nurture such memories, anger will become a poison that contaminates not only our lives but the whole body of Christ.

To try to justify our anger and resentment only brings death to ourselves and God's church. If we care about our emotional and spiritual health and the health of the people of God, we will not let feelings of self-righteousness or a desire for justice or revenge rule us. "Never let the sun go down on your anger." Let's keep to this advice no matter what. We can decide to communicate with others who have hurt us or to forgive them ourselves without letting another day pass. Realistically, some situations or feelings may need a little more time to be fully resolved. But it is best to put resentment, hurt, and anger to rest as soon as possible.

The Desire to Dominate

Anger can be the fruit of a self-centered existence. Many angry people want to be in control of life. They feel safe and secure only when they can control or predict what will happen next. And the only way to insure control is to dominate other people and situations. But they are often frustrated in this desire since life doesn't always comply with their wishes. As a result, they become angry at people and at life in general.

Such thoughts as "She bothers me"; "Why can't they do it right? [meaning my way]"; "This doesn't make me happy" can be our spontaneous reactions to people and things that fail to please us. We become angry when things don't go our way or when our wishes are not considered a priority.

If you recognize yourself in this description, try to answer this question, "Why were you *so* angry?" Could it be because you didn't get your way or because someone made life uncomfortable for you?

It's not always easy to face the truth. But it's essential that we do. The fact is that our problems with anger and with other of our emotions often stem from a self-centered view of life. We have become the most important factor in any situation. The mark of true maturity is the ability to balance our own needs with those of others. Our call as Christians is to model ourselves after our Lord Jesus Christ, who was always primarily concerned for the good of others. Let us have the same concern.

Too Much Pressure

Pressure, fatigue, illness, and premenstrual tension can make us more vulnerable to anger. Too many duties and responsibilities can wear us down emotionally and physically to such an extent that we become angry at the slightest provocation. Such anger indicates that we have reached our "breaking point." When we become ill or over-tired, it's easy to take our frustration out on others. As we have said in an earlier chapter, premenstrual tension often results in irritability or irrational anger. An entire book could be devoted to any of these topics, but I will mention only briefly the role they can play in anger.

When I am very busy and have overextended myself, it's easy for me to become irritable with the children or with anyone who crosses my path. It took me a while to make the connection between pressure and fatigue and irritability. By the end of an especially pressured week I would find myself in tears. It wasn't just the pressure but fatigue as well. I felt terrible for having been so impatient with the children and cross with my husband. Randy would take one look at me and realize that my problem with irritability and anger had stemmed from poor planning on my part. He would point out that I needed to say no more often, or else I needed to eliminate some things from my life in order to make room for the new responsibilities and activities I had taken on.

Whether pressure, fatigue, illness, or premenstrual tension are operating in our lives, we need to adjust our priorities accordingly. If we don't we will constantly be battling a short temper, a sharp tongue, or the desire to administer a resounding spanking to our children, even when they don't deserve it. Sometimes the cure for anger is as simple as rescheduling some things and getting more rest. What a relief it can be to discover that!

Rechannelling Our Anger

We can be tempted to repress our anger in order to avoid sinning. But, as we have said, repression is no answer. What then should we do with our angry feelings?

One constructive approach involves rechannelling our anger into positive behavior. As odd as it sounds, anger can help us develop the fruit of the Spirit if it is properly directed.

For instance, suppose you have difficulty relating to your next-door neighbor. She irritates you no end, and you are always tempted to relate curtly and unkindly to her. Yet you know that such behavior only makes matters worse.

Instead of being ruled by your irritation, you can decide to rechannel the energy generated by your anger into patience and forbearance. You can ask the Lord to help you use it to build your determination to love this woman, by speaking kindly to her, praying for her, and forbearing when she rubs you the wrong way.

Does this sound like repression? It's not. Repression is accomplished by our willpower, while rechannelling our anger can only be accomplished by the power of the Holy Spirit. Patience and forbearance are the fruit of the Holy Spirit, not of our own unaided attempt to change things.

Anyone who has had a problem with anger, whether expressed by temper tantrums or simply by withdrawal—may wonder if they can ever be free of their anger problem. All of us have heard advice like: "If you're angry, count to ten" or "Take it out on something else." But, somehow, such suggestions seem a little weak in the face of the persistent presence of anger. Like any other emotional difficulty, problems with anger have no simple answer. Habit, sin, and stress all contribute to our angry feelings. But, if we depend on the Lord and make a firm decision to change and to exercise self-control, *we can do it!*

It's so hard, Jesus, to understand and control my anger sometimes. But with you, I know that I can have victory. Bless me with a spirit of power and love and self-control so that I can bring my feelings under your lordship. Thank you for the power you have given me.

EIGHT

Depression—A Way Up and Out

DEPRESSED? "NOT ME," you say! But haven't you ever described the way you feel as "blah," "low," "blue"; or, "Sometimes I feel like crying and don't know why"; or, "I'm so tired all the time." If you have, then you may have experienced what is commonly called depression.

Depression ranges from being very mild (feeling "moody" for a few hours) to very severe (feeling hopeless and discouraged for days, weeks, or months on end). Some people claim they are never depressed. But usually this means that they only use different labels, like "blah" or "low," to describe the way they feel. Regardless of what we call it, it's important that we learn to recognize depression. Once we do, we need to learn how to deal with it, particularly if it's become a persistent difficulty in our lives.

Every woman experiences a degree of mood fluctuation in her daily life. Remember, the normal Christian life isn't one in which there's no variance of emotions. It's normal to sometimes feel less than one-hundred percent enthusiasm for life.

Why Christians Suffer from Depression

Christians often experience relief from chronic or low-level depression when they renew their relationship with the Lord as an adult. One woman told me, "When I first renewed my relationship with Christ as an adult, I found that all the symptoms of depression, my old companion, disappeared. I experienced a lightness and joy that had been absent from my life for so long." Faith in Jesus Christ is reason for hope. When we realize that Jesus died for us and when we experience the power of his Spirit alive in us, we have cause to rejoice and be hopeful.

But her story continues. "Gradually, and to my disappointment, my depression began to return, until I felt that nothing had really changed."

Why do Christians still experience depression? Why do some problems seem to go away only to return later? Depression is a symptom which indicates that something isn't working correctly in our lives. I have found that a variety of sources account for the depression that Christians experience. Here I would like to consider six of the most common ones: (1) unrealistic expectations of life and other people; (2) a poor self-image; (3) self-pity; (4) introspection; (5) unrepented sin; and (6) spiritual oppression. (These are not listed in order of importance.) Usually one or a combination of these six are at the root of depression.

Unrealistic Expectations

One of the more subtle causes of depression is rooted in unrealistic goals and expectations. "Psychiatrists tell us that depression does not occur when things are at their worst, but when there is a discrepancy between hope and fulfillment" (Elisabeth S. Weiss, *Female Depression to Contented Womanhood* [New York: Zebra Books, 1977], p. 17). When I first read that statement I couldn't decide whether I agreed with it. But the more I thought about it in light of the cases I've dealt with, the more I began to believe that the psychiatrists were right.

Whatever the reason, most women tend to have some unrealistic expectations for themselves, for other people in their lives, and for the institutions they are involved in. Before you begin to protest this statement, let me explain. In my experience, even some of the most "realistic" and "unemotional" women will admit to holding *very* high standards for their lives and the people in them. Often, their standards are so high that only a super being could ever live up to them. For some women, these high expectations only show up in one or two areas of life, while for others, they may be all pervasive.

Our expectations of other people can also tend to be very high. Whether our parents, husbands, friends, co-workers, priests, or ministers, we often expect others to care for us, to be sensitive to all our needs, and to understand us *instinctively*. We expect them to have within themselves an abundance of love, discernment, and sensitivity, as well as the ability to effectively communicate all these things to us.

If we look at our lives objectively, we may be amused to realize that we have been expecting perfection from, say, our mothers or our husbands. But, on a subjective level, these high standards are the ones by which we actually do gauge their performance. Objectively, we know that our husbands are imperfect. When they come home from work, they may be preoccupied, responding with a simple yes or no to our efforts at conversation. However, we may have built up a picture of how our husbands "should" come home every evening: they should enter with a cheerful smile and then enfold us in a romantic embrace, giving us their undivided attention for the rest of the evening. What they "should" be and what they are can sometimes be entirely different things.

Remember that statement: "Depression occurs when there is a discrepancy between hope and fulfillment," between the "should" and the "what is." This same principle also applies to the circumstances of our lives. We may have very high expectations about the kind of fulfillment and satisfaction we expect from our jobs, marriages, leisure time, and education. For instance, on one level we may be perfectly aware that no job will ever totally fulfill our interests, abilities, and training. But internally, we may still think that our job ought to do all these things for us. The greater the discrepancy between hope and fulfillment, the greater the potential for depression.

Self-Image

Problems with self-image are closely connected with the tendency to hold unrealistic expectations. Consider what you would say if you were asked to make a list of the "shoulds" in your life: what you *should* look like, what you *should* be free to do, what you *should* be able to achieve, what friends you *should* have. If you're like most of us, your list would probably read like a fantasy. It might even conjure up the memory of childhood stories of the beautiful and kind princess who is mistreated and who is later rescued by a brave and handsome prince. Of course they live happily ever after. I've found that most women believe in living "happily ever after." How this will happen, who will be their prince, what predicament they will be rescued from varies from woman to woman.

Our expectations of ourselves can be the "hope." The reality of who we are is often the "discrepancy." Of course I have nothing against living happily ever after—I know I want to. But the important issue is whether our expectations of ourselves and of other people and situations are the right ones. If they are unrealistically high or if they are not from the Lord, every day will be full of disappointment. Such constant disappointment leads to anger or resentment towards ourselves or others. Later on, this disappointment (the discrepancy between hope and fulfillment) will give birth to depression.

Rita, a Christian since childhood, always wanted to have a family of her own some day. Her mother had done everything she could to prepare Rita for marriage. She gave her a hope chest, training in home economics, and so on. After high school, Rita began her first bout with depression. She was lonely at home. She considered her secretarial job monotonous and began to dread going to work each day. The years went on. She was twenty-five and still single. If only she was married, she told herself, her loneliness and depression would disappear. She would be so fulfilled!

When Rita was twenty-nine, she met a good Christian man who loved her sincerely. After their marriage she was glowing and very content. Their first child was eagerly welcomed. But before long, she became depressed. How could this be? She had everything she always wanted. Why wasn't she happy? As we talked, it became clear that her expectations for her husband and for her family life were extremely high. Herein lay the root of her depression. In her earlier fantasy of marriage, she had moved a husband, children, and her own home into the position of "savior" for her life. Once she had these things, *then* she would be happy and secure.

We worked through her super-standards until she was able to form some realistic expectations for her life. We concluded that Jesus needed to be put back on the throne. Only by living totally for him can a woman, single or married, ever be happy and secure.

Once she accepted Jesus as her only savior, she had to face the fact that her husband was a busy, imperfect human being who loved her. And that was all right. She had to let him love her as best *he* could, rather than expect him to be like the hero of a Gothic romance novel. Rita also began to understand that Christian fellowship could be an important life-giving ingredient in her life. In the past, her expectation for marriage had been so high that she never valued other relationships. Now she was free to develop loving, supportive relationships with others.

When she realized that marriage wasn't a magic cure-all for her life, Rita could begin to enjoy the love and security that marriage can bring when it is in the right perspective. Her depression and melancholy faded as the "shoulds" stopped tyrannizing her life.

Here are a few suggestions for handling the "shoulds" in your life:

1. Pray and ask the Lord to help you see and understand the way that "shoulds" operate in your life.

2. Make three lists, marking the first, "self"; the second, "others"; and the third, "circumstances." Then enumerate the "shoulds" that rule your life in each category.

3. Next to each statement, write down what is really going on in those situations. Does the reality match your expecta-

tions of what "should" happen?

4. By yourself or with the help of a friend begin to formulate more realistic expectations.

5. Decide to substitute realistic standards for the unrealistic ones in your life.

Self-Pity

Another major contributor to depression is self-pity. It creates, renews, and enhances feelings of depression, hopelessness, and discouragement. This testimony from a mature, responsible Christian woman describes how self-pity and depression worked in her life.

Depression is one area that I had a problem with for a long time. Most people probably didn't know this because I never made it very obvious. But under the surface, I was always depressed. I thought I was stuck with this problem for life. I had hoped that it would go away once I got married, but it didn't. That dismayed me. Here I was, married and still depressed. It really scared me. I realized then that it was *my* problem. It wasn't the circumstances of my life but something going on inside of me.

I knew that the problem was a serious one and that I needed to do something about it. I tried to rebuke it and repent of it. I prayed about it, talked to people about it, and did anything else I could think of. Nothing seemed to make much difference. Then one of my friends gave me a book about depression written by a Christian author. After many years of counselling, the author had concluded that every form of depression is caused by self-pity. That hit me very hard, like a boulder.

"Now, wait a minute," I thought. "I don't feel sorry for myself; I don't get into self-pity." But after praying and thinking about it, I realized that I did pity myself, in very subtle, self-righteous ways. I would say to myself, "I really deserve better than this; I've worked hard; I've given up a lot, and I think I deserve a better situation than this." Or, "I deserve a better job than this." These kinds of thoughts ran through my mind frequently. I probably wouldn't say them out loud, but only to myself. When I was single, I would plead with the Lord, "Why am I not married?" Or, "Why haven't you given me a husband?" I may not have put it quite so blatantly, but that's how I felt. In a very subtle, self-righteous way, I felt sorry for myself. I never recognized that my self-pity was at the root of my depression.

I had never known what to do about depression, but I knew how to handle self-pity. I knew I needed to repent of it. I decided not to attack the depression but to start fighting off the self-pity. Every time I began to feel sorry for myself, I admitted my self-pity, repented of it, and received God's forgiveness for it. What an incredible difference this made for my life! I began to realize that I didn't have to be bound by the depression. I could overcome it by overcoming my self-pity. My experience has taught me that I need to be careful when I talk to others who are having difficulties. I want to listen sympathetically, but I don't want to encourage self-pity. Instead, I want to bring them the Lord's light, to give them his perspective rather than to commiserate with them about the unfortunate circumstances in their life.

Clearly, self-pity can be a major source of depression. It can take a variety of forms. Here are a few of the more common kinds of self-pitying thoughts that could run through a woman's mind:

If my mother had only taught me good eating patterns when I was young, I wouldn't have a problem with my weight now. (What a poor victim I am!)

I would probably be married and happy by now if only *that* hadn't happened. (Poor me!)

My husband is a big disappointment to me. We can't afford the kind of house we want because he's just not making enough money. (How I suffer!)

If I hadn't had so many children, life would be different for me now. (Sigh!)

These are just a few of the thoughts that could run through our heads. Difficult situations do occur, and we should not expect everybody and everything, including ourselves, to be perfect. We should be on the alert for any thoughts that could be concluded with "poor me" or, "What a victim I am in this situation." Like the woman in the previous example, we can try to justify our self-pity. It can become "righteous" self-pity. But self-pity is never righteous. Self-pity is a sin. It denies the power of the cross, the fact that God saved us and is still saving us. If we believe that life follows its own reckless course, without the direction of a loving Father, then we have cause for self-concern, to take things into our own hands, and to feel sorry for ourselves. But the world is not just running amuck. God himself has his hand on our lives. No matter how terrible things seem, he is still present to us. He has not left us orphans but has given us his Holy Spirit to enable us to handle our difficulties and trials with more power as Christians.

A Sin against Hope

"We know that God makes all things work together for the good of those who have been called according to his decree" (Rom 8:28). That means that nothing will happen to us that will not work for the good. Often, Christians misinterpret this passage to mean that every situation that happens to us will be good. That's not true. That's not quite what scripture says. It says, "God makes all things work together for the good of those who have been called." The most terrible human tragedies can happen to us; we may suffer mental anguish and disappointments that in themselves may not be good by any stretch of the imagination. But God *can* work that suffering for the good. And that is the hope to which we are called. That's why it's wrong to pity ourselves. Self-pity is a sin against hope. If we indulge in it, we are not hoping in God.

But we need to place our hope in him, not in ourselves or our circumstances. Paul says, "What then shall we say to those things, if God is for us, who can be against us?" "He who not even spared his Son, Jesus, but has delivered him up for us all, how can he fail to grant us also all things with him? Who shall make accusation against the elect of God? It is God who justifies, who shall condemn? It is Christ Jesus who died, yes, and rose again, he who is at the right hand of God, who also intercedes for us" (Rom 8:31-34). How can we, even for a moment, entertain the thought that God would withhold something good from us? He sent his own Son to assume our flesh and die for us. Is he going to change his mind now and decide that it really wasn't worth the effort? Of course not.

Patience

I should say something here about patience. Patience is intimately connected to hope. Notice what Paul says to the Romans: "For in this hope we were saved. Now hope that is seen is not hope. For who hopes for what he sees? But if we hope for what we do not see, we wait for it with patience" (Rom 8:24-25). Paul is speaking about the hope that comes from knowing that we are adopted children of God, waiting for the fulfillment of our inheritance. All creation is groaning, awaiting the revelation of the sons of God.

Paul also speaks about hope for things we do not yet see or have. Isn't that how we experience many situations in life? We do not see how things can work together for the good right now. We cannot see how this marriage will work for the good; we cannot see how being single is working for the good; we cannot see our present financial situation ever working for the good. It all looks like nothing but tragedy. But it is not tragedy. Because the Lord is in charge.

Paul also says of hope that "we wait for it with patience." Often lack of patience gives rise to self-pity. We know what we want, and we want it *now*. Fortunately, God doesn't work as we do, responding to our impulses and our need for immediate gratification. In his time, all things will work for the good. His hand is on us; his promise has been made to us. We need to await it with patience.

"But I'm Different"

Another thing that contributes to self-pity is the feeling that, somehow, we or our situation are unique. With that in mind, we tell ourselves that scripture's teaching does not apply to us right now. In our eyes, our difficulty, suffering, disappointment, or discouragement are unique to us. We cannot quite believe that our suffering is something common to all men. This approach feeds self-pity.

Paul says in Romans, "Who shall separate us from the love of Christ? Shall tribulation, or distress, or persecution, or famine, or nakedness, or peril, or sword?" (Rom 8:35). Let me reword it in modern American speech. "What can depress us? Shall marriage crisis, or being unmarried, finances, inflation, or recession, or not enough clothes, or discipline problems with the children separate us from the love of God?" Verse 37 says, "But in all these things we overcome because of Him who has loved us." We haven't overcome because of our strength or holiness, but because of *him*. "For I am convinced that neither death, nor life, nor angels, nor principalities, nor things present, nor things to come, nor powers, nor height, nor depth, nor any created thing, will be able to separate us from the love of God, which is in Christ Jesus our Lord" (Rom 8:38-39). Paul doesn't leave much to the imagination. He pretty much covers everything, doesn't he? Neither height, nor depth, nor anything created will be able to separate us from the love of God which is in Christ Jesus our Lord.

Passivity

Another aspect of self-pity is passivity. Sometimes we are not willing to assume responsibility for our lives. Often we see ourselves as the victim of our circumstances or the victim of our emotions. We need to be more aggressive instead of just sitting back and saying, "poor me" and "isn't it rotten that this is happening to me." In this case, to be aggressive in the right way means to go before the Lord, confessing our sin of self-pity to him. It even helps to say it out loud. There's no hiding when you say aloud, "Forgive me for pitying myself." Once you've repented, accept God's forgiveness and seek him for his mind in the matter. Sometimes he will require us to *do* something about a difficult situation. A passive attitude only reinforces the negative aspects of a situation. The Lord may be offering us the grace to do something to make a difference.

Introspection

Introspection is another important factor in depression. Here is a testimony from a woman in her late thirties who has been a Christian for ten years.

Something was going on inside of me the other day. I was confused and a little depressed. So I went to my prayer time and said, "Oh Lord, I just don't know what's going on here; I just don't get this. Everything seemed fine and then I felt all this confusion and depression." Then I said, "Wait a minute. So what if I don't understand this? It's just my feelings here. And I do know that Jesus is Lord and that he is worthy of praise. So why am I wasting my prayer time thinking about what is going on with me? Why don't I just praise the Lord?" Later that day I began to think about how I used to handle such situations, years ago. Often I would spend my whole prayer time trying to figure out why I was depressed, what was going on with me. This only made me more depressed and confused when I should have been praising the Lord and giving glory to him. He is always worthy of praise, despite how I feel. I know I can let him take care of whatever is going on with me. Now I don't spend that much time thinking about myself. I spend a lot less time being introspective, thinking about how everything is affecting me. I know that there is a direct correlation between my depression and the amount of time I spend being introspective.

I think this woman's experience says a lot. Introspection makes way for depression and distracts us from loving and serving God. The way to be free from lingering depression is to make a conscious decision to turn to Jesus when we pray, focusing our attention on him and on the needs of others, rather than on ourselves.

Unrepented Sin

Depression can also be a symptom of unrepented sin. Most psychology books don't mention sin as a source of depression because they have explained away its existence. I often wonder how many men and women who undergo years of counselling, analysis, and hospital treatment for depression would find great relief simply by admitting their wrongdoing and accepting the love and forgiveness of God.

Although emotions like depression can be defined as reactions or feelings, they are often symptoms which indicate that something isn't working right in our lives. When we commit a sin and try to minimize it, rationalize it, or justify it, we step out of a right relationship with God. The Lord is holy and he calls us to be holy. Only by being a holy, righteous people can we enjoy the fullness of our relationship with God. Emotional health is a fruit of that relationship. He will not allow us to continue to grow and flourish while we are separated from him by sin. Depression, anxiety, fear, guilt, and self-hatred are some of the feelings that may accompany separation from God through sin.

Psalm 32

Some psalms in scripture are known specifically as penitential psalms. Psalm 32 is one that illustrates the relationship between sin and depression particularly well. One translation entitles the psalm "The Joy of Him Whose Sins Have Been Forgiven." It is a psalm of David.

Happy is he whose fault is taken away,
  whose sin is covered.
Happy the man to whom the Lord imputes not guilt,
  in whose spirit there is no guile.

As long as I would not speak, my bones wasted away
  with my groaning all the day,
For day and night your hand was heavy upon me;
  my strength was dried up as by the heat of summer.
Then I acknowledged my sin to you,
  my guilt I covered not,
I said, "I confess my faults to the Lord,"
  and you took away the guilt of my sin.

For this shall every faithful man pray to you
  in time of stress.
Though deep waters overflow,
  they shall not reach him.
You are my shelter; from distress you will preserve me;
  with glad cries of freedom you will ring me round.

Many are the sorrows of the wicked,
  but kindness surrounds him who trusts in the Lord.
Be glad in the Lord and rejoice, you just;
  exalt, all you upright of heart.(Ps 32:1-7, 10-11).

Let's take a look at verses three and four: "As long as I would not speak (repent) my bones wasted away with my groaning all the day. For day and night your hand was heavy upon me; my strength dried up as by the heat of summer." David describes his emotional and physical state, the direct consequence of a serious sin that he had not yet repented of. David had committed adultery with Bathsheba and then murdered her husband Uriah. At first he tried to hide his sin from the Lord.

As long as he persisted in his sin he was plagued with depression, guilt, and sickness, but once he admitted his sin and repented, he could rejoice. The psalmist describes the fruits of repentance as happiness, gladness, freedom, kindness, joy, and exultation. All of these are natural consequences of living a righteous life.

We fail to repent of our sins for several reasons: (1) The sin has become so habitual that we have become dulled to it (gossip, critical and judgmental thoughts, problems with our in-laws). (2) We rationalize our sin, saying, "Everyone does it" (being greedy for money and success). Or we say, "It's not a sin anymore" (premarital sex). Or, yet again, "I had to do it" (have an abortion because I couldn't have this baby). (3) Our pride stands in the way. It's not easy to humble ourselves enough to say, "I did wrong; will you forgive me, Lord?" Pride can make us do anything but repent.

To correct this failure, we need to ask the Lord if: (1) there is any sin in our lives that is so habitual that we no longer see it; (2) we have rationalized or justified our sins; or (3) our pride is preventing us from coming before the Lord. Once we recognize the sin, we need only ask our Father to forgive us. And then we need to receive his forgiveness.

> Not according to our sins does he deal with us,
>   nor does he requite us according to our crimes.
> For as the heavens are high above the earth,
>   so surpassing is his kindness toward those who fear him.
> As far as the east is from the west,
>   so far has he put our transgressions from us.
> As a father has compassion on his children,
>   so the Lord has compasssion on those who fear him.
>
> (Ps 103:10-13)

Knowing that God has forgiven us, we need to accept his forgiveness. After we've been forgiven, we don't need to go back and repent again. We don't need to go around feeling sorry for ourselves that we are such terrible sinners. We need to put our sins as far from us as the east is from the west. That's how far God has put them away from us. We don't need to stir up bad feelings or more repentant feelings.

Next, we need to decide not to sin anymore. The true fruit of repentance is the determination to turn away from sin in the future. Once we have decided to sin no more, we are ready to turn to the Lord, firmly established in our new state of forgiveness. Our natural response to the Lord's forgiveness should be to praise him for his goodness and mercy. In fact, worshipping God for his perfect love and kindness is an important element of repentance.

> But the kindness of the Lord is from eternity
>   to eternity toward those who fear him,
> And his justice toward children's children
>   among those who keep his covenant
>   and remember to fulfill his precepts.
> The Lord has established his throne in heaven,
>   and his kingdom rules over all.
> Bless the Lord, all you his angels,
>   you mighty in strength, who do his bidding,
>   obeying his spoken word.
> Bless the Lord, all you his hosts,
>   his ministers, who do his will.
> Bless the Lord, all his works,
>   everywhere in his domain.
> Bless the Lord, O my soul! (Ps 103:17-22)

A Christian doctor once shared with me his insight into the role that sin can play in illness.

> One patient, 64 years old, had never been free of multiple symptoms during the eight to ten years I knew her. She exhibited concern about her blood pressure, abdominal cramps, skin rashes, shortness of breath, insomnia, nerves, bowels, and so on.
>
> I think her real problem may have been chronic anxiety

and depression due to her unwillingness to forgive her former husband. After a few years of marriage, her husband had left her and obtained a divorce. She slowly became embittered toward him. Although she professed to be a believing Christian, and was prayed with many times, she refused to forgive her former husband.

When I mentioned this to her, she would not even decide to *want* to forgive him. I made it clear that I thought she would be locked into her symptoms unless she forgave him. But she still refused. As far as I know, she hasn't gotten any better.

While this may seem like a dramatic example, many Christian doctors and counselors recognize the significant relationship between repentance and health—physical, emotional, and spiritual. Not every physical or emotional difficulty stems from unrepented sin. But it is worthwhile to investigate anxiety and depression as possible symptoms of unrepented sin.

Negative Speech

How and what we talk about can have a big effect on our emotions, particularly on depression. Claudia, for example, is in her early thirties and has a chronic problem with depression. The Christian counselor who worked with her recognized that there was a direct link between what she talked about and her emotions. Claudia was in a weekly sharing group with some other Christian women in her neighborhood. She had a habit of thinking negatively about nearly everything. And she shared her negative thoughts and feelings with anyone who would listen. She felt that she was simply "being in the light."

Claudia and her counselor decided to take a different approach. They agreed that she would not talk about her problems as much as she had been. When she was asked how she was doing, she wouldn't respond by saying, "Oh, I've been struggling with this for a week, and I'm really discouraged because of that." Instead, she agreed to first share at least three good things that the Lord had done for her or three positive experiences she had had during the week. Only then could she mention one difficulty that she had been having.

After a while, Claudia began to realize that a large portion of her waking time was spent talking about how depressed she was or about how terrible her circumstances were. At first it was very difficult for her to control her speech. But her decision to speak positively eventually made a tremendous difference in her life. Her faith in God's power to help her grew stronger. Her speech, mind, and emotions had all been working against her to create feelings of depression and self-pity. Now they could begin to work *for* her.

Spiritual Oppression

While self-pity, introspection, and sin all contribute to various forms of depression, the spiritual realities can not be ignored. It would be naive not to consider a few of the spiritual facts of life. Depression is a primary area in which the evil one hassles Christians. If feelings of discouragement and hopelessness still persist when handled in light of the wisdom presented in this chapter, it's time to take some spiritual authority over those feelings.

Emotions can be artificially stimulated by evil spirits. When our feelings and circumstances don't seem to match up, we need to take up our spiritual weapons. Jesus has given us authority over the powers and principalities. But we must exercise it. A simple command, "Any spirit of hopelessness (despair, etc.) affecting me, I command you to leave in the name of Jesus."

Often we will experience immediate relief. We will wonder why we didn't take authority over the evil one sooner. At other times we may need to persevere in the spiritual assault that we have launched against the forces that work against us. We may need to ask a brother or sister to join in the assault with us. When it comes to spiritual warfare, persistence and patience pay off.

Practical Suggestions

When you begin to feel depressed, try to stop yourself as soon as you realize it. Ask yourself, "When did this begin; what was I thinking about; what precipitated this depression?" If you do that for a week or so, you may begin to see a pattern and you may be able to identify the source of your depression. Perhaps it is something as simple as having too much free time on your hands or lacking clear-cut goals. Or it may be the effect of some negative conversations you've had. Perhaps your depression started when you began to compare yourself with a person that you have always felt inferior to. These things can set off a chain reaction resulting in depression.

Once we understand how people and circumstances can affect our emotions, we won't be caught off guard and we won't be bewildered at the emotions that have been stirred up. As we do this, our life and our emotions will become much more predictable. We will be strong enough to handle them in the right way. We may still have to face that fellow worker who seems to do his best to belittle us. But we will be able to work with what we *know*. If we don't know what causes us to despair, to become hopeless and discouraged, we will always be on the defensive with our emotions.

It's a good idea to talk to someone who is a mature, reliable Christian if you suffer from more than mild depression. It can be difficult to identify what is wrong and what you should do to change things, especially when life looks so bleak.

Take care of yourself! Get good sleep and eat nutritionally balanced meals. Remember, your body can contribute to feelings of depression. Fatigue and inadequate food only fuel a downward cycle. Continue to wash and fix your hair and take care in dressing. Giving up is a tempting solution, but it will only contribute to feelings of hopelessness. Set simple goals daily and weekly. When left to routine it's easy to lack interest in going on. Make yourself keep going by setting manageable goals for the day.

Exercise is important. If you usually enjoy tennis, running, or other active sports, do them with someone if you can. If you normally don't engage in sports, you may find it refreshing to take regular, vigorous walks. Exercise can help you fight the inertia that depression can bring.

Finally, pray and read scripture. Paul tells us that we are to take the word of God as a sword to fight the enemy. Knowing God's truth and God's promises enables us to engage confidently in battle. It enables us to be victorious. Here are some scripture passages that can help us do battle.

—Psalms 33, 42, 43, and 71 speak of the kind of hope we are to have in our God.
—Lamentations 3, particularly verses 21-33, speaks of a downcast man who nevertheless relies on the steadfast love of the Lord.
—1 Peter 1:13-21 proclaims the faith and hope we can have in God through Jesus Christ.
—John 5:13-15 speaks of the fruit of our confidence in God.

We should read these and similar passages daily, reminding ourselves of God's truth. We should refuse to let feelings of hopelessness and discouragement rule the present and the future. For it is the truth that sets us free!

My moods seem too big for me to handle sometimes. But I know, Lord, that you have not left me on my own. You have given me your light to pierce the darkness of my discouragement and depression. Come, Lord Jesus, my hope is in you.

NINE

True and False Guilt—Freedom versus Bondage

So MANY DEDICATED Christians live in bondage because they lack a clear understanding of how to handle the guilt feelings they experience. We are supposed to feel guilty if we've sinned. Such guilt can act as a signal to us that we've done something wrong. It can be the first step of repentance. But, often, we feel guilty even when we haven't done anything wrong. Let's explore the difference between true and false guilt.

Believe it or not guilt is a gift from God to his people. Like other of our emotions, it can be a tool for physical, emotional, and spiritual health. There are three parts to this particular tool: conviction, repentance, and reconciliation.

Conviction spotlights our separation from God. Sometimes by nudging us gently, other times by shouting loudly, guilt tells us that we have done wrong. It not only points out our sin, but it urges us to repent and be reconciled with God. Conviction is the knowledge that by thought, word, action, or lack of action, we have sinned. We have not lived in accordance with the commandments of God and of his church. We feel guilty about our wrongdoing. Guilt feelings can be like the red light on the car dashboard that signals that something is wrong. We don't have to be a trained mechanic to know that we should stop and take care of the problem.

But our feelings of guilt do more than inform us. They are designed to move us to repentance. The knowledge or experience of sin should motivate us to acknowledge our sin or wrongdoing, not only to ourselves but to God. If we truly repent, confessing our sin and returning to God, then our guilt has functioned as God intended. Guilt without repentance is guilt malfunctioning. If we fail to heed guilt, we will be like the driver who chooses to ignore the red light on the dashboard. By continuing to drive the car, despite the warning, he usually compounds the original problem by putting further stress on other parts of the car. If we ignore our guilt, we will continue to be separated from God. We will be deprived of the grace made available through repentance to strengthen us to avoid further sin.

We know that if we acknowledge our sin and turn to God for forgiveness, he will graciously receive us. He will remove the obstacle that sin created in our relationship with him. Through the fruit of repentance and reconciliation, we will no longer experience the consequences of sin; we will no longer be separated from God. When we confess our sin ("I sin, Lord") and repent ("forgive my sin"), we will be able to forgive ourselves and enjoy the fullness of a right relationship with God.

Several psalms stand as examples of true penitence. They can teach us how to come before the Lord with a truly contrite heart. My favorite psalm concerning sin and reconciliation is Psalm 103, in which the psalmist shows a true understanding of the fruit of repentance.

> The Lord works vindication
>   and justice for all who are oppressed.
> He made known his ways to Moses,
>   his acts to the people of Israel.
> The Lord is merciful and gracious,
>   slow to anger and abounding
>   in steadfast love.
> He will not always chide,
>   nor will he keep his anger for ever.

He does not deal with us according to our sins,
    nor requite us according to our iniquities.
For as the heavens are high above the earth,
    so great is his steadfast love toward
        those who fear him;
as far as the east is from the west,
    so far does he remove our transgressions
        from us.
As a father pities his children,
    so the Lord pities those who fear him.
For he knows our frame;
    he remembers that we are dust.

As for man, his days are like grass;
    he flourishes like a flower of the field;
for the wind passes over it, and it is gone,
    and its place knows it no more.
    But the steadfast love of the Lord is from everlasting to everlasting
        upon those who fear him,
        and his righteousness to children's children,
    to those who keep his covenant
        and remember to do his commandments.

False Guilt

While some guilt feelings indicate the presence of sin in our lives, not all of them stem from that source. Some Christians suffer from an overly sensitive or scrupulous conscience. These Christians are hyper-aware of every weakness and sin. And they experience deep guilt from things that are not sinful. This kind of guilt clouds our true relationship with God. Unfounded guilt is spiritually and emotionally oppressive. It commonly stems from three sources: human imperfection, sins of the past, and temptation.

Many of us confuse simple human imperfections—mistakes

and inadequacies—with sin. Often, good Christians punish themselves emotionally for making a mistake, for not knowing something, or for forgetting. I know many women who have lived for years under such a burden of guilt. Some of their guilt feelings can be traced back to parents, teachers, or clergy who made them think their shortcomings, limitations, mistakes, or temptations were sinful or wrong.

Stacy, a busy woman of forty, had a very strict childhood. Her parents emphasized perfection in every area. Externally she seemed a confident, successful woman, but internally she wrestled constantly with guilt feelings. She felt guilty if someone didn't like her ("Maybe I could have done something differently") or if she were a few minutes late ("I'm really terribly sorry") or if she couldn't be best at something (First place meant you were a good person. Second or third meant you did something wrong).

Stacy knew that something was wrong with the way she perceived life. Eventually, she realized that she felt guilty about any sign of weakness, mistakes, or limitation. She equated these things with sin, with not living up to God's expectation of her. To correct this, she studied what scripture actually said about sin and availed herself of the help of a Christian counselor. She gained a new freedom in accepting her human condition as she realized that it was all right to be imperfect. No one but Jesus Christ ever lived without sin. As Stacy accepted herself, repented of true sin, and concentrated on the Lord's love and goodness, she found new spiritual and emotional energy.

Past Sin

Past sins can torment good Christian men and women. Guilt feelings over sins that have already been repented of and forgiven present an insidious obstacle to a free and growing relationship with the Lord. Feeling "dirty" or unworthy because we have sinned in our past only makes us vulnerable to a kind of emotional and spiritual oppression never intended by God. Our guilt feelings are often reinforced by the idea that it is more virtuous to continue to "feel bad" about our sins even after we have repented. But the contrary is true. Continuing to feel bad about past sin that we have repented of only obstructs our relationship with God.

Consider Margaret, a Christian wife and mother of three children. Margaret had an abortion as a teenager. Although she had repented numerous times for consenting to an abortion, she couldn't shake a pervasive feeling of guilt and condemnation. She felt that because of her past she could never *really* be close to God. She was sure that she had committed an unforgivable sin and could only stand on the fringe of God's people, looking in.

Margaret needed someone with a knowledge of God's mind to help her overcome her self-condemnation and guilt. This is how we proceeded. We agreed that abortion was wrong and against God's will for the human race. Then we got on our knees and she admitted it, repented of it, and received God's forgiveness. Afterwards, she agreed that she *never* had to repent for it again. She acknowledged that God forgives us generously whenever we admit our sin before him.

Now for the hard part. The next time she began to feel condemned and alienated from God because of her abortion, she had to rely on the truth (part of the armor of God that Paul refers to in Eph 6:14). Margaret had done a scripture study on God's forgiveness and had written appropriate scripture verses on individual index cards. Whenever she felt troubled by guilt feelings, she would read as many cards as she needed until she felt that she knew the truth again. In this case, the truth was that she was forgiven and that she lived in loving union with God. When she knew the truth concerning forgiven sin, she subordinated her feelings of guilt, condemnation, and self-hatred to that truth. She decided to *believe* scripture rather than her feelings, because her feelings simply were not indicating the truth concerning God's forgiveness and love. Forgiving ourselves is sometimes harder than accepting God's forgiveness. But hating ourselves is only an obstacle to moving on in the Christian life and appropriating God's forgiveness.

Temptation

Temptation can be another source of false guilt. Many Christians confuse temptation with sin. While yielding to temptation is a sin, *temptation is not in itself a sin.* Even so, we often feel guilty about our temptations or feel responsible for them. I've known good Christians who were unable to discern this type of false guilt from true guilt. All of us may occasionally experience temptations to be dishonest or we may have sexual dreams or we may desire to hurt someone. These temptations are an unfortunate part of our human condition. They result from sin and Satan in the world. But it's no sin to experience temptation.

Another woman, May, wrestled with an underlying sense of guilt and separation from God. During our conversations together, we uncovered the root of her difficulty. Like many Christians, May never grasped the difference between temptation and sin. She felt personally responsible for any temptation she experienced, and many of her temptations had to do with the area of sexual desires. After a while, she was able to discern between temptation and sin. She realized that all Christians experience temptations. She wasn't responsible for the temptations but only for yielding to them.

When May felt guilty about having a strong desire to masturbate or engage in sex outside of marriage, she learned that it was her responsibility to resist those temptations and turn to the Lord for the grace she needed. If she did that, she needn't feel guilty. In her effort to control her sexual desires, May decided to become a better steward over her thought life. She found that she was greatly fortified by resisting thoughts that would stimulate her, not reading books or magazines which focused on sex, and not getting into situations where she might weaken and yield to temptation.

Jesus himself experienced strong temptation prior to the start of his public ministry. While fasting in the desert, Satan came to him tempting him with food, power, riches, and glory. What did Jesus do? He resisted the evil one and turned to scripture for the truth. We need to deal with temptation the same way he did. Most of us wish that temptations would never come our way. When they do come along, we may fight them more vigorously at one time than another. But temptation is not sin, and we do not have to feel guilty about it.

Discernment

How can we learn to distinguish between true guilt and guilt feelings? For a start, we need to realize that there is a knowable, objective standard of right and wrong. God has revealed that standard in scripture and has helped us to understand it through the teaching of the Christian church. Once we learn to recognize sin, we can identify feelings of guilt that stem from a source other than sin.

Beware of the evil one. He is determined to destroy the benefit that true freedom from guilt provides. He is known as the "accuser of the brethren." Remember that the Holy Spirit convicts us of sin in order to bring us closer to God. But the burdens of guilt rarely draw us closer to the Lord as his daughters. The evil one would like nothing more than to impede our relationship with God. Command the accuser to be gone in the name of Jesus.

If you have difficulty distinguishing sin and wrongdoing from other factors that contribute to feelings of guilt, I strongly suggest that you seek help from a priest, minister, Christian counselor, or an older sister in the Lord. It's especially important to do this if guilt has become a strongly established pattern in your life. But exercise wisdom when choosing someone to confide in. Decide on someone who operates out of a strong, traditional, scriptural base. Unfortunately, some church leaders and counselors have adopted a secular theology which has concluded that the Ten Commandments are no longer "relevant" or "meaningful" to the modern Christian.

Once we realize that some of our guilt feelings are not only inappropriate but destructive to our emotional and spiritual well-being, we will need to actively rid our lives of them. To do this, we will need to have some clout, some answer, ready when we meet up with those guilt feelings. We can start by deciding to have the truth, rather than our feelings, rule our lives. I know this is easier said than done, but we cannot afford to let our feelings act as a standard of right and wrong. If we do, we are only asking for trouble.

One very practical and specific way to combat destructive guilt is to collect 3x5 index cards on which you have recorded key scripture passages. These can help you be objective about the truth, especially when your feelings threaten to overwhelm you. When you begin to feel guilty about something, reach for your cards to remind yourself of the truth.

The Love of God—A New Focus

Much can be said about guilt and about advising Christians in regard to guilt. But when all is said and done, the key to freeing ourselves from destructive guilt is to know the love of Jesus Christ. The whole of the Christian life springs from the love of God. It is God's love that gives us life. He it is who has given us his son Jesus out of love for us. His love gives true joy and security. We need to immerse ourselves in God. We can do that by coming to a fuller knowledge of him. It isn't enough to simply know the do's and don'ts of the Christian life. Our experience is to be much richer. We are to know, at a fundamental level, that God is love.

Many people take a negative approach to the Christian life, focussing on what Christians aren't supposed to do. Let's take a more healthy and positive approach, focussing on our personal love relationship with God. That way, the do's and don'ts will fall into proper perspective.

One way to come to a fuller knowledge of God is to consider the images he uses to describe himself in scripture. He is the Good Shepherd who cares for his sheep. He is the Father who with an open and forgiving heart welcomes the son who turned from him.

Your love, Father, is all I need. Teach me again and again about your loving kindness and forgiveness. For I long to be one with you. May my heart be formed according to your word.

TEN

Anxiety and Fear— A Modern Epidemic

T WO THOUSAND YEARS ago Jesus said, "Do not be anxious." He knew that men worried chronically about what they would wear, what they would eat, about their future and their health. Human nature hasn't changed much over the years. We worry about the same things today. Although we have seen tremendous technological advances, amazing medical break-throughs, and significant advances in education, we continue to worry about health, clothes, food, and security. The standard of living has increased greatly, more people are living longer, and social security and unemployment benefits are available as never before. Yet we are more anxious and fearful than ever.

Statements like: "I'm just a worrier"; "So many things are uncertain that I lay awake at night and worry"; "My stomach is in knots" indicate what an anxious people we are. We worry about ourselves, about others, about the past, the present, and the future. What if I get into a plane crash? What happens if my husband gets sick? What happens if my child dies? What if we have another financial depression? What if I become ill? What if we can't buy the house we want? These kinds of thoughts and feelings have become so acceptable in our society that you can hardly tell the difference between Christians and non-Christians when it comes to anxiety.

If we were without the Lord and left to our own devices, there would be plenty to worry about. We would not just be imagining things. The world seems to be heading on a crash course for financial disaster. Inflation is spiralling and recession has set in. Political and social unrest and insecurity are more evident than ever before. The suburbs are no longer the havens from crime that they once were. Cities are beset by mugging, rape, and looting. The arms race is accelerating. World powers have nuclear weapons that could wipe out whole nations and leave the world devastated for many years to come. When we look at the world around us, we find no lack of cause for worry and fear. It isn't just our overactive imaginations at work. Death, sickness, financial ruin, and overall uncertainty about the future are real conditions.

Should the Christian be concerned about these things? Don't we also have to deal with inflation and recession, the nuclear arms race, sickness and death? Yes, of course! Christians have to deal with all of these things. It's not our troubles that make us different but our response to them. We need to know and proclaim the Christian perspective for handling difficulty in our lives.

The fact that God exists and that he is who he says he is, is cause enough to change the fundamental way we perceive life. He is the Lord of Lords, the creator and sustainer of the universe. Nothing can happen to any of us that God cannot handle. He is big enough for any of our problems.

On an intellectual level we might assent to this fact. But unless we have a personal, daily awareness of who God is and what he has done for us, we will be no different than non-Christians. We need to know that our security lies in God alone. It doesn't lie in our bank account or in our good health. Our security and peace do not depend on whether or not we can control different situations in our lives. It must be rooted in Jesus Christ himself. He is in control. We need to know that his death and his resurrection have meaning and power for our lives today.

Trust in God

Let's take a moment now to review this passage from Matthew's Gospel.

For this reason I say to you, do not be anxious for your life, as to what you shall eat, or what you shall drink; nor for your body, as to what you shall put on. Is not life more than food, and the body more than clothing? Look at the birds of the air, that they do not sow, neither do they reap, nor gather into barns, and yet their heavenly Father feeds them. Are you not worth much more than they? And which of you by being anxious can add a single cubit to his life span? And why are you anxious about clothing? Observe how the lilies of the field grow; they do not toil nor do they spin, yet I say to you that even Solomon in all his glory did not clothe himself like one of these. But if God so arrays the grass of the field, which is alive today and tomorrow is thrown into the furnace, will he not much more do so for you, O men of little faith? Do not be anxious then, saying, "What shall we eat?" or, "What shall we drink?" or, "With what shall we clothe ourselves?" For all these things the Gentiles eagerly seek; and your heavenly Father knows that you need all these things. But seek first His kingdom and His righteousness; and all these things shall be added to you. Therefore, do not be anxious for tomorrow; for tomorrow will take care of itself. Each day has enough troubles of its own. (Mt 6:25-34)

In this passage, Jesus reveals important characteristics of his Father. And he describes the relationship that the Father has with us, his children. Jesus communicates that God is not an impersonal creator who, having set the world in motion, says to each of us, "Good luck, honey. Let's see what you can make of the life I've given you." The images that Jesus uses here very clearly portray a Father's loving care. "Look at the birds of the air, that they do not sow, neither do they reap, nor gather into barns, and yet their heavenly Father feeds them. Are you not worth more than they?" That wasn't really a question. He was saying, "Gloria, Mary, Karen, you are of much more worth than the birds of the air. You scarcely notice their presence in the trees and on the ground. Yet my Father in heaven is aware of their very life, and he provides for them. And look at the grass of the field, and the lilies of the field. Aren't they beautifully cared for by the same Father who cares for you?"

Jesus then says very specifically that we are not to worry about what we shall eat, or what we shall drink, or what clothes we shall put on. "For all these things the Gentiles eagerly seek." These are just the things that non-Christians are always striving for. As God's children, we don't need to be like non-Christians, who spend so much of their waking time and energy worrying about what's going to happen to them. "What is going to happen to my teenage son?" "What is going to happen to my rebellious teenage daughter?" "What is going to happen to my three-year-old child, who has a congenital birth defect?" "What is going to happen to my husband, who has a drinking problem?" "What is going to happen to me financially in the future?" The Lord never says that problems won't be a part of our lives. They happen and they happen regularly. But we turn to the Father; we seek first his kingdom and his righteousness, and all that we need will be given to us.

As we develop a love, trust, and faith in God and in his power for our lives, difficult things will not make us anxious, nervous, or worried. We will approach all things with faith. But how can we do this?

We should go on our knees to our Father, remembering who it is that we worship. Many Christians pray to God, not quite convinced that he is big enough for their lives and for the people they love. To combat our doubts, we should read scripture in order to stir up faith within us by reminding us that we have not merely a competent God, but a God who is all-powerful. He is big enough for every situation in our lives.

Who Is Our God?

Many of us seem to think that God is interested only in our spiritual life. We expect him to reveal himself to us in prayer, but we don't expect him to break through into the practical aspects of our daily lives. The truth is that we don't have an uninterested or impotent God. He is aware of us. He loves us and knows what we think and what we do, when we sit and when we stand. God is not a senile father, who is generally benevolent towards us but fundamentally unable to accomplish anything in our lives. We come before him on our knees, remembering that he is the King of Kings and Lord of Lords. As such, he has power over everything that he has created, in the heavens and on the earth.

Besides being the powerful, supreme ruler over all of creation, God is a loving Father to us. We need to remember that he made and sustains the universe and that, wonder of wonders, he is also our Father. He is personally interested in our lives and concerned for our well-being. He can bring the same power by which he holds the stars in the heavens, the moon in the sky, and keeps the earth rotating on its axis to bear upon the things that concern us in our small lives. Psalm 139 states that he knit us in our mother's womb, and he was aware of our days even before they were counted, before they were numbered.

As we approach difficulties in our lives, we can put first priority on loving God and seeking his kingdom. Remember that he who made the promise is worthy of trust (see Heb 11:11). He *will* meet our needs!

Taking Stock of Your Life

Let's examine our lives and take stock of how we are doing. Do we suffer from fear; do we entertain anxiety; do we worry about many things? Anxiety expresses itself uniquely in women, though men suffer from it too. I want to offer three descriptions of anxiety that point out that all anxiety does not spring from the same source. If we are to overcome our anxiety, we must know and understand the source of it. Only then can we apply the right measures of faith and correction necessary to eliminate anxiety from our lives.

Anxiety-Love

We often equate anxiety with the love of family and friends. If we love someone, we will worry about them. If we love our husbands, we will worry about them; if we love our children, we will be anxious about their lives; if we love ourselves, we will worry about our future.* Anxiety rules under the banner of love and can easily become a tyrant on the throne of love.

It's not always easy to know how to love someone. It's not easy to know how to love your husband, your children, or even yourself. Anxiety can become a handy outlet for your love. At least you feel like you are doing something by worrying. For example, if your husband's job is in jeopardy, and you can't do anything about it, it's easy to say, "At least I can worry about it."

Another way we can express anxiety-love is by being overly concerned about the physical health of our families. We can over-medicate, over-dress, and over-protect our families. We can become overly concerned about feeding them just the right foods. Of course it's good to do what we can to insure the health and well-being of those we love. In fact, it's our responsibility to do so. But our concern often becomes exaggerated.

The same pattern of over-concern can develop when it comes to loving ourselves. A career woman's concern for her future may intensify as she sees the years pass by. She becomes anxious about what will happen to her. Will she get that next promotion? Her healthy self-love has become distorted by self-concern and anxiety. She worries about herself, her health, her finances, and her future. What will happen in ten years, in twenty years?

If anxiety has become an expression of love for us, it's time we learn to divert our love into more constructive channels. We need to deal with anxiety-love head on, to admit that there are more helpful ways to show our love and concern.

Young girls often learn from their mothers that loving and worrying go hand in hand. Hasn't everyone heard that "it's a mother's right to worry?" Though our mothers were probably good women, their way of expressing love and concern may not always have been the most helpful. Expressing love through anxiety is a difficult habit to break. Ask yourself whether your own expressions of love, especially "motherly" love, are exhibiting symptoms of anxiety. (By the way, you don't have to be a mother to fall into this trap!)

Be a Woman of Faith

The key to overcoming anxiety is to become a woman of faith. We should replace anxious expressions of love with a growing confidence and assurance that the Lord loves us and is in charge of our lives. We are not left alone to grapple with the forces of life. As in everything, the Lord will supply the grace and strength for us to continue living for him if we begin to take steps to remedy our difficulties. Remember Matthew 6:33, "Seek first his kingdom and his righteousness, and all these things shall be yours as well."

The opposite of an anxious woman is a woman of faith. At the core of this woman is her trust in God. No matter how bad things look, she firmly trusts and hopes in God. Her hope doesn't spring from naivete or from irresponsibility. Neither is she overly spiritual. She is a woman who, because of her great love for God, has chosen to base her life on God's promises in scripture. *Chosen* is the key word. It's not that some women are born with faith, while others are not. We can stir up and encourage faith through the choices we make. We can decide not to let fear, doubt, anxiety, and insecurity rule our lives. We can choose to live every day hoping and trusting in God.

If we are to be women of faith, like Sarah, Abraham's wife, or Mary, the mother of God, we need to fill our thoughts with hope and trust in God; we need to speak about people and situations in a way that proclaims the rule of God in our lives. We can choose to act in a way that reflects our fundamental alignment with the promises of God in scripture.

No, it's not beyond your reach. You'll find that it's easier to have faith in Jesus when you've decided to live a life of love, trust, and hope in God. The more you decide to trust God in specific situations, the more your assurance of God's faithfulness will grow.

Intercession

I've found that women experience more peace in their lives if they direct their concerns to the Lord. Are you concerned for *y*our children or your parents? I am. I want the best for my parents and my own family. Sometimes I see their need so clearly that it hurts. But instead of letting fear for their future or anxiety for their well-being gnaw at me and preoccupy my thoughts, I spend a special time on my knees interceding for the specific needs I see in their lives. I often pray in a more general way, commending the person or situation to the Lord, believing firmly that he knows their needs even more clearly than I do.

The key is to *leave* your concern with the Lord when you rise from prayer. Remember Christ's words, "What father among you, if his son asks for a fish, will instead of a fish give him a serpent. . . . If you then, who are evil, know how to give good gifts to your children, how much more will the heavenly Father give the Holy Spirit to those who ask him!" (Lk 11:11-13). When we are tempted to take back that burden of love, we need to remind ourselves that our Father hears our prayers and loves those whom we love even more than we do. We can trust him for ourselves, for our husbands, for our parents and friends.

Rose shared with me an experience from her life that bears on this point.

Somehow, I always thought that I needed to be anxious if I were really going to be a good wife and mother. One day I heard a talk that said, "You don't have to be anxious." That just stopped me in my tracks. It has become a word of freedom for me.

If we were having guests, I would worry: "Does the house look all right? Will I be comfortable talking with the guests if my husband isn't in the room?" I thought that if you cared, you worried. Now I've learned that I don't have to worry in order for a situation to work out. I can rest in the Lord and make the best effort I am capable of. He will prepare me, giving me the right words at the right time. Many things have changed in my life since then. I am happier and so are the people around me. In fact, the years since I first heard those words, "You don't have to worry," have been the best years of my marriage.

Anxiety-Control

Not all anxiety is motivated by misguided love. Sometimes people can be anxious out of a sense of self-protection or a desire to maintain control of a situation. In their search for security, many women attempt to control or manipulate the lives of other people or situations in order to make sure that the "right" thing happens. This is particularly common when a woman does not have direct responsibility for a situation. She may use anxiety as a means to manipulate whoever is in charge.

Perhaps a woman is concerned about her family's finances. In fact, she's downright worried and fearful. Her husband makes an adequate salary, but inflation has definitely affected their lifestyle. He has told her that his salary is sufficient for their needs. They will have to do the best they can to cope with inflation.

However, the wife disagrees with her husband's assessment of the situation. As she sees prices rising, she begins to worry: "What if inflation rises higher next year? Will we be able to have a vacation? Will we be able to buy the kinds of Christmas presents that we have been accustomed to? Will we be able to purchase the new living room furniture that we have been saving for?" Consequently, her anxiety about the future only increases. Soon, her conversations with her husband are dominated by her anxiety. She communicates rather indirectly at the breakfast table that before long they won't be able to afford eggs for breakfast (she sighs audibly), hitting him where it hurts. When he comes home at night, she asks if his boss has said anything about giving him a raise. She does this despite the fact that she knows that the boss is probably not going to say anything about a raise because the company is in a difficult financial position. As the days and weeks go on, her anxiety places a sure and steady pressure on her husband.

Obviously, the wife is trying to change her husband's initial decision by pressuring him through her anxiety, even though she may not be fully conscious that that's what she's doing. There are two probable outcomes. First, her husband will begin to withdraw more and more from her; they will argue more frequently, and he will tell her that he doesn't want to discuss the family's finances anymore. Short of getting angry, he may just withdraw from her, eating quickly, leaving the house sooner, coming back later, listening to the radio or the television more frequently (with the volume up). Or, second, his wife could finally get to him. She has successfully applied enough emotional pressure to change her husband's initial decision. At last he goes to his boss, against his better judgment, to ask for a raise. Or he takes on a weekend job even though he doesn't think it's necessary.

Now this isn't an extreme case. I have known many women for whom anxiety has become a frequent tool of manipulation. Mothers often manipulate their children. They worry about them so much that the children finally give in to their mothers to avoid the pressure they feel from their mother's anxiety. Married women are not the only ones who use anxiety as a tool for manipulating others. Many single women use it, as well, to manipulate friends, parents, or other relatives. The aim of this type of anxiety is to directly or indirectly influence people or circumstances. It is motivated by selfishness, though we may try to rationalize it by reasoning that we really know what's best in a given situation.

This type of anxiety is habit-forming. Why? Because it works so well. Its very effectiveness reinforces our desire to use it. Of course we may not even be aware that we are using anxiety as a tool to manipulate others until it becomes so rooted in us that it's hard to shake. Some of us have probably already become masters at indirectly ruling and controlling whole families, decisions, and situations.

The drive for dominance is very strong in many women. Often these women compulsively attempt to dominate or control people and situations. This compulsion, expressed through anxiety, actually stems from a basic lack of security. Such women rarely feel secure in their relationship with the Lord and with other important people in their lives. If we recognize ourselves in this description, what can we do about it?

I don't recommend that we simply swallow our concerns, never voicing them to anyone. If a situation has the potential to make us anxious or fearful, we should communicate our feelings to the person who is responsible for the situation. If a woman is concerned about her family's finances, she should communicate her concerns clearly and responsibly to her husband. But she shouldn't tell her friends and neighbors how worried she is. After all, they have no power to change her family's financial picture. On the other hand, she shouldn't simply hold everything inside. A woman who never says anything can be eaten away with anxiety. Refraining from speaking about concerns is not a sign that someone is free from anxiety. It is healthy to communicate concern to those who are responsible, to those who can do something about the situation. We should communicate our concern directly rather than indirectly, stating it once or twice but not constantly repeating it. Even though we may have a sense of immediacy about something, we should not continually apply pressure on other people. After doing this, we can exercise what we've been learning about being a woman of faith.

Anxiety-Distrust

This type of anxiety stems from a lack of trust and faith in God and in others. We may think that past experiences justify our distrust. "I never really expect God to help me. I prayed that my little brother would get well, but he died. I decided then that I could never really trust God." All of us have been hurt by people and situations in the past. Why should we risk trusting the Lord when he might fail us?

But scripture tells us that God *never* fails us. Perhaps the problem is with our perception of our circumstances, rather than with God's action or seeming inaction. Of course there are no easy answers to some of the suffering we experience or see others experience. But we must cling to our belief that God is who scripture says he is. Let us read and meditate on his word to discover more about who he is, and let us ask for eyes of faith, that we may perceive the truth. We can decide to begin trusting God. As we let him be our Savior, our rock, we will grow in our ability to trust him.

Even if a single woman has no one in her life to be a source of security, she can be a woman of faith and trust in the midst of a storm. A married woman does not have to base her security on the fact that her husband is a perfect Christian and a perfect spouse. Her security can be rooted in her trust in God and his power for her life. The world is not running out of control. God is in control and she is in his hands. Hallelujah!

Most of us would jump at the chance of getting rid of our anxiety for good. As we begin to identify which of the three types of anxiety operate in our lives, we may be faced with the realization that anxiety has become a habit for us, one that isn't easy to break. But we can make a major beginning by applying self-discipline, trust in God, and intercessory prayer. We should also repent if we are guilty of manipulating other people and situations.

Anxiety and Our Minds

Our thought patterns often give us the most difficulty when it comes to anxiety. They can be compared to a river, carved deeply into the face of the earth. Suppose someone wants to use the river to irrigate some land. They would begin by diverting the river to a more helpful course. At first, things would be pretty messy. The river would often flood the surrounding area, depositing mud and debris everywhere. At that stage the riverbed wouldn't be deep and sure enough to contain the river under all conditions. But, later, it would become as established in its new course as it had been in its old.

Something similar happens to us when we try to change our thought patterns. Our thinking tends to run along comfortable, familiar grooves. It takes the path of least resistance. If we have made a habit of thinking in fearful or anxious ways, we should realize that such thoughts have run nice little niches in our minds. When a situation that has made us fearful in the past presents itself, our minds automatically click into their old thought patterns. And our anxious thoughts produce anxious emotions and behavior.

Have you ever had thoughts like these: "What if I can't handle it?"; "What if my husband is killed in a tornado on his way home?"; "What if I forget my speech at the meeting tonight?"; "What if my child's fever leads to convulsions?"; "What if this ache in my knee is the first sign of crippling arthritis?" Our speculations can go on and on. But they do nothing to prepare us for the future. In fact, anxious thought patterns only work against our ability to prepare for the future. Worrying has never changed anything for the good. Anxiety has never prevented an accident, prolonged a life, spared someone pain, or generated money. Anxious thoughts result in hand-wringing, pacing, headaches, knots in our stomachs, over-talkativeness, and insomnia. Anxiety is an affliction that can make us difficult to live with as it spreads to and affects others.

If we are to change, we will need to commit ourselves to expending the kind of time and energy that it takes to transform our patterns of thought. Right now our anxious thoughts run in habitual patterns. They may not always be pleasurable, but they are comfortable. Such thoughts come as an automatic reaction, one that doesn't take any effort or energy. When we are tired or caught off guard, our minds, our behavior, and our emotions will flip to the most familiar patterns rather than to the right ones. In order to change, we must be willing to count the cost demanded of us. But we should also remember that we are not left on our own. The Lord himself will help us.

If you are determined to change, you will need to be patient with yourself. It can be very difficult to uproot old patterns of thinking. It will take time to establish new thought patterns and new reactions to replace the old ones. You will need to fight discouragement. At the first failure, you will be tempted to say to yourself, "I knew it was impossible; I'm just too fearful." Or, "This is too big for me to handle." You may be right. Perhaps the situation is too big for you to handle. But remember that you have a Father who is big enough to handle it. If you have faith, he will provide the grace you need in order to have a renewed mind.

Fear

Fear can either be helpful or destructive in our lives. You will remember that I pointed out earlier that fear can work to protect us from potentially harmful situations.

We could compare fear to a guard dog. If a dog is well-trained, it can serve the members of a family by protecting them and their house from intruders. Heroic dogs have even been known to save the lives of their masters or of children at risk to their own lives. But a dog that has been trained to attack or intimidate others but lacks the complementary training of discipline and obedience is a potentially destructive force.

When fear is not contained and disciplined, it begins to rule our lives. Fear of the future, fear of people, fear of the dark, fear of heights, fear of death, and so on, all indicate that destructive fear has taken charge of our lives. These fears and many more begin to dictate our actions. Before we know it, our fears determine what we will and won't do. We no longer have the internal freedom to choose. Like anxiety, fear refuses to stay confined to a small area of our lives. If we let it roam at will, it will usually claim more and more territory.

An example from my own life may help to illustrate the role that fear can play in our lives. I am generally a confident woman, who does not have to struggle much with fear. Several years ago I had a close brush with the kind of fear that can rule a person's life. During the winter I attended a class one evening a week. Since I needed to put the children to bed before I went off to class, I often arrived late. The parking lot was quite a distance from the school, and I began to dread that long lonely walk from the car to the building. My imagination conjured up pictures of what could happen in the dark lot. Once I got to the school, any sudden noise would send me running to the building. What if someone was waiting behind one of the cars? What if I got raped? What if . . . ?

As the winter progressed, my fear of being alone or in the

dark or in parking lots slowly increased, until I noticed that fear had taken hold of my life. I began to experience low-level anxiety earlier and earlier the day of the class, and when I was alone at other times during the week strange noises or the approach of unfamiliar cars would alarm me.

I began to realize that I had a bona fide case of uncontrolled fear on my hands. Finally, a little embarrassed, I confessed to my husband the fear that I had been struggling with.

This is the strategy we developed to deal with it:

1. First of all, we recognized the truth. The kind of fear I was experiencing was, for the most part, destructive. It wasn't part of God's plan for my life, and I didn't have to put up with it.

2. My fear did serve a useful function by indicating that I should take more precautions at night. I would either park closer to school or arrive earlier so I could walk in with the other students.

3. I needed to deal with the destructive fear by asking the Lord to give me victory over this bondage.

4. I needed to take authority over any work of the evil one. He likes nothing better than to see God's people be fearful.

5. I needed to take authority over my thoughts. I agreed not to imagine any more "what if's." As I anticipated my evening class, I would focus on the class itself. As I drove out to the school, I would turn my thoughts to the Lord and praise him for his goodness.

6. I needed to discipline my reading habits and to control my television-viewing better.

This last decision wasn't easy for me. When my husband first suggested that I needed to be more careful about what I read or what I watched on television, I was insulted. I told him that I wasn't a child and that I could handle it. But I did notice that the newspaper usually carried several articles about women being attacked or raped. And women's magazines often featured articles detailing a woman's experience with physical attack. Television carried special programs on rape and its effects. Detective shows and movies sometimes portrayed women being mugged (in the dark, in a parking lot?). After a little reflection, I had to admit that my husband was right. I followed his advice and became more selective in my reading and television-viewing habits. After a few months, I noticed that my imagination was no longer running wild. There was less to feed it. The things that I exposed myself to in books, magazines, television shows, and movies directly affected my emotions.

Anxiety and Fear

The Lord wants us to be able to control our fear so that it can serve a useful purpose in our lives. We need to take the appropriate action, sometimes with the help of others, to make certain that fear operates as an obedient servant, not a tyrant. We should recognize that some anxieties are often symptoms of other, larger fears. Anxiety about our health may be a superficial expression of our fear of death. Our anxiety over the closeness of our family ties may mask a deeper fear of being rejected or abandoned.

One of the best ways to deal with fear and anxiety, especially when they have become a large and regular part of your life, is to initially limit your efforts to one or two areas. Don't attack every area of anxiety and fear in your life at once. That's not very good strategy. If you were fighting a war, you would first assess your enemy's strength. Then you would assess your own strength and the power at your disposal. Having done this, you would be in a much better position to deploy your forces in the most effective way. You would be able to identify which enemy targets to attack first. That way, you wouldn't risk spreading your forces too thin.

It's like that with our emotional lives as well. If we try to do too much at once, we will only fail and become discouraged. Instead, we should aim at winning several small victories in order to build up our courage.

Identifying Your Fears

To be able to overcome fear, you need first of all to recognize it. Begin by keeping a notebook especially set aside for this purpose. List a few fears that you feel up to facing. Write down specific fears that you have, the situations that evoke them, and most importantly, the truth about how to get free from them.

Column One: Identify some of your fears and anxieties. If you have difficulty doing this, ask yourself what things you tend to speculate about, to ask "what if" questions about.

Column Two: Identify people, things, situations, and thoughts that stimulate your fears.

Column Three: Write down the truth that you know applies to the situation. Search scripture for God's mind about these things.

I've drawn up an example (p. 140) of what a page in your notebook might look like. As you become more adept at identifying and overcoming habits of anxiety and fear, you may have more to record in column three about what you have learned.

The Role of Scripture in Fighting Fear

In order to fight fear we actually need to perceive the situation as a fight. We need to be willing to fight through to victory even as we begin to experience fear.

We need to arm ourselves with the spiritual armor that Paul speaks of in Ephesians. "That is why you must rely on God's armour, or you will not be able to put up any resistance when the worst happens, or have enough resources to hold your ground.

"So stand your ground, with truth and integrity for a breastplate [Do what you need to in order to be responsible in the situation.], wearing for shoes on your feet the eagerness to spread the gospel of peace [The joy of God residing in your

Sample Notebook Page

Fear/Anxiety	Stimulates Fear/Anxiety	The Truth
1. Fear about my health or my family's health	1. Magazine article and television shows that focus on tragedy, disease, and death 2. Minor aches and pains that I have 3. Conversations centering on illness, hospitals, or death.	1. My fear and worrying cannot cure, prevent, or safeguard me or my family. 2. Only the Lord is my rock and my shield, my fortress, and my health. 3. I need to avoid reading about death and disease simply out of curiosity. 4. Scripture passages: Matthew 6:25-34; Luke 12:22-31; John 14:1; Philippians 4:6-7.
2. Fear of rejection/ insecurity	1. Being around "popular" people 2. Being around people who do anything well 3. Going to parties 4. Forming new relationships	1. The world's standard of perfection is not my standard or God's standard. 2. The Lord made me in his image and likeness and I am loveable. 3. My confidence comes from being a daughter of the King. 4. I will remember my list of strengths and decide to accept compliments from others, believing them to be true. 5. Scripture passages: Hebrews 4:16; Psalm 34; Psalm 139.

heart and mind will being forth the light of Christ.] and always carrying the shield of faith so that you can use it to put out the burning arrows of the evil one [You need to be well-equipped with strong faith and trust in God in order to resist the attacks of the evil one]. And then you must accept salvation from God to be your helmet [Salvation from God is his power and his strength. You need to accept that his power makes a difference in your life.] and receive the word of God from the Spirit to use as a sword" (Eph 6:13-17).

We should memorize scripture so that when we are most vulnerable, when we are in the midst of fighting the good fight, we have some ammunition in our minds and hearts to use against the enemy. That way we won't have to try to remember where the passage is in scripture. Many of us don't know the word of God very well. Often, I will speak to other women about the promises that the Lord made in scripture. It's not unusual for them to respond by acting as though they're hearing these promises for the first time. They wonder why they can't remember those passage when they read them.

If we want to complete our armor, we should begin to memorize scripture passages that can be a protection for us. God has given us the power to live a righteous and victorious life. We often get into trouble by not taking advantage of the power available to us. The word of God should not be a stranger to us; it should be constantly on our minds, in our hearts, and on our tongues. Here are some scripture passages that I've found to be particularly helpful in overcoming anxiety and fear.

Psalm 22	Psalm 73	Jn 14:1
Psalm 23	Is 40-60	Phil 4:6-7
Psalm 27	Jer 17:7-8	Heb 4:16
Psalm 33	Mt 6:25-34	Heb 11:1-3, 6
Psalm 34	Mt 8:23-27	Heb 13:5-6
Psalm 37	Mk 4:36-41	Jas 1:5-6
Psalm 46	Lk 8:22-25	Pt 5:7
Psalm 50	Lk 12:22-31	
Psalm 55	Lk 21:34	

God wants us to have peace, courage, and faith in all the difficult circumstances of our lives. But we need to cooperate with his grace if we are to experience these things.

Lord, I want to be a woman who trusts you. Teach me how to overcome my fears and anxieties. Sow in me a spirit of trust and hope in you. For you, Lord, are worthy of all my trust.

Conclusion

A GOOD RECIPE usually requires several ingredients in order to bring out the full flavor and aroma of the food. The difference between a good meal and an excellent meal has to do with the right blend of the proper ingredients. Too much salt in a soup or sauce makes you wish you had a gentler touch on the saltshaker, while too little salt leaves the meal flat and bland.

Most of us know that to cook anything well, we need to be patient, taking time to understand the balance of ingredients. What role does yeast play in bread-making? What is the relationship of yeast to sugar in the bread? Understanding the role and balance of different ingredients gives us more confidence in our cooking.

Ideally, a meal of vegetables, meat, herbs, and seasoning will produce a harmony of taste and smell. When we walk into a kitchen with a good spaghetti sauce simmering, we say, "That smells great!" We don't say, "That tomato sauce, basil, oregano, garlic, and bay leaf smells good."

Believe it or not, dealing with all the different factors that go into a stable emotional life is similar to cooking well. A number of factors—our relationship with the Lord, our self-image, and good stewardship over our minds and bodies—contribute to a healthy emotional life. When we have difficulty with our emotions, a number of factors can all work together to overcome destructive emotional responses.

Similarly, many factors in our emotional life all merge together to produce the fruit of the Holy Spirit: peace, patience, joy, kindness, love, goodness, faithfulness, gentleness, and self-control.

It's easy to swallow the bait of "easy answers" and "miracle principles." They are often guaranteed to transform us instantly.

Sometimes these promises sound more like advertising slogans for weight reduction plans. Doesn't "Apply these life-changing principles and your depression will disappear" sound suspiciously like "pounds and inches off in twenty-four hours"?

In my experience, the answers to our difficulties are rarely that simple. I have seen God perform miracles in people's lives. But in order to sustain the miracle or the healing that he has begun, these people have needed to bring a number of things in their life into better order. Perhaps they have needed to repair relationships, repent of sinful habits, discipline themselves, and grow in holiness in their thoughts and speech.

Does this sound beyond you? Don't worry. None of us can achieve this ideal through our own effort. Only by being women who rely on God for their holiness can we ever be holy or healthy. We need to have patience with ourselves, with others, and with God's timing. A popular song years ago was entitled "You Can't Hurry Love." Nor can you hurry anything that will last. Things that last take time, commitment, and the work and power of God.

We can't hurry God's work in us. Much of what needs to happen in our lives comes as the fruit of living the Christian life. All fruit takes time to grow. When we don't seem to change fast enough, we must do our best to fight discouragement and to stir up faith in God and his purpose in our lives. The fruit of the Spirit comes from walking, speaking, and loving in God's way.

When we have had a chance to apply all the principles presented in the preceding chapters, who will we see when we look in the mirror? We will see an imperfect woman, a woman who is on the way, who has decided to cooperate with the grace of God. But, more and more, we will see the woman God intends us to be—a woman of faith, a woman who loves God above all things. Remember, that woman is *you*.

Books for Christian Women from Servant Publications